Developing
Literacy Skills

Sheila Hales

Heinemann Educational Publishers
Halley Court, Jordan Hill, Oxford OX2 8EJ
A division of Reed Educational and Professional Publishing Ltd

OXFORD MELBOURNE AUCKLAND
JOHANNESBURG BLANTYRE GABORONE
IBADAN PORTSMOUTH (NH) USA CHICAGO

First published 2000

04 03 02 01
10 9 8 7 6

ISBN 0 435 102788

Designed and typeset by Hart McLeod, Cambridge

Printed and bound in Spain by Edelvives

Original illustrations ©Heinemann Educational Publishers 2000

Illustrations by Gary Swift, Paul McCaffrey courtesy of Sylvie Poggio;
David Cuzik, Alan Wade, Jeff Anderson and Bob Harvey courtesy of Pennant

Tel: 01865 888058 www.heinemann.co.uk

Introduction

This book gives you a wide range of text types to read and enjoy. These include fiction extracts, poems, drama extracts, adverts, leaflets and extracts from information books. The texts are arranged in thematic sections so that you can compare writing on different topics.

Each of the texts is followed by activities and support material. There are **Questions** to help you to check that you have understood the text and to help you to understand different levels of meaning in it. There are **Investigations** which ask you to look closely at the language of the text. These will show you how a writer achieves a particular effect. Finally, there is a **Response** section which asks you to write your own text or create your own piece of drama. Each of these sections is supported by help and check boxes to give you the hints and tips you need to complete the activities.

There are many different types of text in this book: some are funny, some are serious. However, they have all been chosen because they are interesting to read and discuss. I hope that you enjoy reading them.

Sheila Hales

Contents

ACKNOWLEDGEMENTS

The publishers gratefully acknowledge the following for permission to reproduce copyright material. Every effort has been made to trace copyright holders, but in some cases this has proved impossible. The publishers would be happy to hear from any copyright holder that has not been acknowledged.

Extract from 'Horribly Silly Stories' by Michael Rosen, published by Kingfisher. Reprinted by permission of Peters Fraser & Dunlop Group Limited, on behalf of Michael Rosen. ©Michael Rosen.

Extracts from 'Skellig' by David Almond, published by Hodder and Stoughton Limited. Reproduced by permission of Hodder and Stoughton Limited.

Extract from 'Harry Potter and the Philosopher's Stone' by J. K. Rowling, published by Bloomsbury. Copyright ©J. K. Rowling 1997. Used by permission of Christopher Little Literary Agency.

Extract from 'D I Y Mummy' published by Dorling Kindersley Limited. Reprinted by permission of Dorling Kindersley Limited.

Extract from 'Cartoon Films' by Rhoda Nottridge, published by Wayland Publishers.

'Drama Lesson' from 'Schools Out' by Gareth Owen, published by OUP. Copyright ©1998 by Gareth Owen. Reproduced by permission of the author, c/o Rogers, Coleridge & White Ltd, 20 Powis Mews, London W11 1JN.

'Growing Up' from 'Collected Poems' by Gareth Owen, published by Macmillan Children's Books. Copyright ©Gareth Owen 1985. Reproduced by permission of the author, c/o Rogers, Coleridge & White Ltd, 20 Powis Mews, London W11 1JN.

Extract from 'The Fwog Prince' by Kaye Umansky, published by A & C Black (Publishers) Limited. Reproduced by permission of A & C Black (Publishers) Limited.

Advert for *Extra Time*. Reproduced by permission of KJC Games.

Extract from 'Twenty Names in Crime' by Andrew Langley, published by Wayland Publishers.

Extracts from 'Stop Them Taking Your Bike for a Ride' and 'Crime together we'll crack it' logo, reproduced by permission of the Home Office.

Extract from 'The Beano' ©D C Thomson & Co Ltd. Reprinted by permission of D C Thomson & Co Ltd.

'What I Watch' by Carol Vorderman, taken from the 'TV Times'. Used with permission of IPC Syndication.

Advert for Shoot Boardgame, from 'Shoot – July 31st 1999' ©Shoot/IPC Syndication. Reproduced by permission of IPC International.

Extract from 'Tama Gotcher' by Robert Dawson, published by Heinemann Educational. Reproduced by permission of Laurence Pollinger Limited.

Extract from 'Bugsy Malone' by Alan Parker, published by Collins Educational. Reprinted by permission of National Film Trustee Company Limited.

'Applemoon' by Rose Flint, taken from 'Every Picture Tells a Story'. Reprinted by permission of the author.

Extract from 'Coming to England' by Floella Benjamin, published by Pavilion Books. Reprinted by permission of Pavilion Books Limited.

Extract from 'Bog Bodies' by Natalie Jane Prior, published by Allen & Unwin 1994. Reproduced with permission of Allen & Unwin, Australia.

Extract from 'Lost for Words' by Elizabeth Lutzeier, published by OUP. Reproduced by permission of Oxford University Press.

Extracts from 'Zlata's Diary: A Child's Life in Sarajevo' by Zlata Filipovic, translated by Christina Prichevich-Zoric (Viking 1994, first published in France as *Le Journal de Zlata* by Fixot et éditions Robert Laffont 1993) Copyright ©Fixot et éditions Robert Laffont 1993. Reproduced by permission of Penguin Books Limited.

'Baby-K-Rap Rhyme' from 'No Hickory No Dickory No Dock' by Grace Nichols (Viking 1991). Reproduced with permission of Curtis Brown Ltd, London, on behalf of Grace Nichols. Copyright Grace Nichols 1991.

Extract from 'The Secret Diary of Adrian Mole Aged 13¾' Sue Townsend, published by The Random House Group Limited. Reproduced by permission of The Random House Group Limited on behalf of Sue Townsend.

'The Sea' from 'Complete Poems for Children' by James Reeves, published by Heinemann. ©James Reeves. Reprinted by permission of the James Reeves Estate.

Extract from 'Raider' by Susan Gates, published by OUP. Reproduced by permission of Oxford University Press.

Section A
Different Worlds

The pieces of writing in this section are all different. There is poetry, fiction and non-fiction. But they are all about worlds that are different to ours. Some of them are real, such as the world of the ancient Egyptians. Some of them are not real, such as the world of wizards. But all of them show us something new and exciting.

In this section, you will learn about:

- nouns
- sentences
- verbs
- punctuating direct speech
- using paragraphs.

A1 About the Authors

The two pieces of writing below are taken from the beginning of two books. Each of them tells you about the book's author. Michael Rosen writes poetry and stories and David Almond writes stories.

Extract 1: Michael Rosen

Whose Book is This?

Michael Rosen was born. When he was young he was a boy, though now he is a man. He's been collecting jokes and silly stories for many years. He catches them with a large net and puts them in little cages on the window-sill and under the table. His house is now full of jokes and five

5 of them are children. They collect jokes too, but most of them are too rude to mention.

Word Bank

ancient: very old
dilapidated: in need of repair

Extract 2: David Almond

About the Author

I grew up in a big family in a small steep town overlooking the River Tyne. It was a place of ancient coal mines, dark terraced streets, strange shops, new estates and wild heather hills. Our lives were filled with mysterious and unexpected events, and the place and its people have given me many of my stories. I always wanted to be a writer, though
5   I told very few people until I was 'grown up'. I've published lots of fiction for adults, and I've won a number of prizes. I've been a postman, a brush salesman, an editor and a teacher. I've lived by the North Sea, in inner Manchester, in a Suffolk farmhouse, and I wrote my first stories in a remote and dilapidated Norfolk mansion.

Writing can be difficult, but sometimes it really does feel like a kind of magic. I think
10 that stories are living things – among the most important things in the world.

 ## Questions

1. Read Extract 1, which describes Michael Rosen. Which of the sentences below are true and which are false? If a sentence is false write down what the truth is.

    a) Michael Rosen has written books for years.

    b) Michael Rosen has four children.

    c) His children think collecting jokes is a waste of time.

    d) Michael Rosen collects stories and keeps them in a net.

    e) Everything in Extract 1 is serious.

2. Read Extract 2, which describes David Almond. Find the answers to these questions.

    a) Where did David Almond grow up?

    b) What four jobs has David Almond done apart from being an author?

    c) Where has David Almond lived?

    d) How did the place he grew up in help him find stories to write?

    e) Why does David Almond think writing is special?

3. Now think about the answers you have already given. Use them to help you complete the two sentences below. Make sure you give reasons for your opinions.

    a) I think Michael Rosen has written about himself in a much *funnier/more serious* way than David Almond because...

    b) I think David Almond's book is likely to be *funnier/more serious* than Michael Rosen's because...

Investigations

1. Look at the chart below. It shows some of the **nouns** in each extract. Check the help box to make sure you know what a noun is. Then find the rest of the nouns in each passage.

Help

A noun is a word which names a person, place or thing.

My <u>children</u> collect jokes too. → person

I grew up in a small <u>town</u>. → place

He catches them with a large <u>net.</u> → thing

Extract	Line	Nouns
1 Michael Rosen	1	Michael Rosen, boy
	2	man, jokes, stories, years
	3	net, c...
	4	w..., t..., h..., j...
	5	_____
	6	_____
2 David Almond	1	family, town, River Tyne
	2	place, mines, streets, shops, estates
	3	hills, lives, events, place
	4	p..., s..., w...
	5	_____
	6	_____
	7	_____
	8	_____
	9	_____
	10	_____

There are two main sorts of noun:

- **Common nouns** are the names of everyday objects such as *man*, *street*. Common nouns always begin with small case letters.

- **Proper nouns** are the names of unique objects such as *Michael Rosen*, *River Tyne*. Proper nouns always begin with capital letters.

2. First check that you have understood the difference between the two sorts of noun. Put the nouns below into two groups: common or proper nouns.

Robert	hair	Manchester	bus	coat	Olympic Medal

3. Make a list of five common nouns in Michael Rosen's passage (Extract 1).

4. Make a list of all the proper nouns used in David Almond's passage (Extract 2).

5. Both the authors have written in **sentences**. Read Michael Rosen's passage (Extract 1) to help you change the information below into three rules for writing in sentences. Remember to read the title of the passage as well.

You should *always/never* begin a sentence with a capital letter.

A sentence *always/sometimes* makes sense.

Sentences *always/sometimes* end with a full stop.

Response

Imagine that in 20 years' time you have become a famous author. Write a short, serious, description of your life and work. Make yourself sound interesting so people will want to read your books. Write about 50 words.

You may like to organise your work like this:

- say when and where you were born
- describe anything interesting you have done (remember you can make things up)
- say what sort of things you enjoy writing
- say where you get your ideas from.

Check!

Make sure that you begin every proper noun with a capital letter and every common noun with a small case letter.

Make sure you write in complete sentences. (Follow the three rules you made.)

This extract comes from Sticky History Books: *Egyptian Pyramids and Mouldy Mummies*. In it, you will find out how to mummify a body.

D.I.Y. MUMMY (DON'T READ THIS UN

1 Take 1 dead body. Lay it on a high table, so you don't get backache bending over it.

2 Wash it well.

3 Shave off the body hair. You can leave the hair on the head if you like.

4 Make a cut (called an incision) in the dead person's side.

5 Hack out the heart, lungs and intestines. Empty out the intestines. This is a smelly job, but don't worry - your workshop is a long way from houses and shops. Clean out the inside of the body with special chemicals.

6 Remove the brains by poking a long, thin hook - a bit like a crochet hook - up through the nostrils and into the skull. Wiggle the hook about a bit until you loosen the brains.

7 Twist the hook and yank the brains out. This means you will not damage the face. You will damage the brain, but this does not matter. Clean out the inside of the skull with special chemicals. There must be nothing left inside the body that can rot. You can leave the eyes in place; they will dry out naturally.

SS YOU HAVE A STRONG STOMACH!)

8 Place the stomach, brains, lungs and intestines in special pots called Canopic jars. Seal the jars. Keep the heart separate - you will need it later.

9 Put the body in a bath of natron (a salt made up of sodium and carbon) for at least 40 days. While you're waiting for the natron, make three coffins.

10 Take the body out of the natron and wash it again.

11 Fluff out the inside of the body with linen and bags of sweet-smelling spices.

USELESS INFORMATION - HEART AND SOUL

To the ancient Egyptians, the heart was the centre of all thoughts and feelings. You could go to the next world without a stomach or brain, but your heart had to be inside your body. Could this be the origin of the old saying, "His heart's in the right place"?

Put a funeral ask over the face. d jewels and ulets to taste.

13 Wrap the body with bandages coated in resin (sap from pine trees) and sweet-smelling spices.

12 Pop the heart inside the chest and stitch the body up again.

Questions

1. Read the questions below and then choose the correct answer.

    a) Why is the workshop a long way from houses and shops?

        i)   so they can empty out the intestines

        ii) because of the special chemicals

        iii) because the job is so smelly

    b) Why is the heart put back in the body?

        i)   because the heart is the centre of all thoughts and feelings

        ii) because you need your heart to get to the next world

        iii) because you can go to the next world without a brain or stomach

    c) Why must there be nothing left inside the body?

        i)   so that the eyes will dry out naturally

        ii) so that there is nothing to rot

        iii) so that the brain will come out

2. Which of the sentences below are true and which are false? If a sentence is false, write down what the truth is.

    a) You must shave the hair off the head.

    b) Emptying out the intestines is smelly.

    c) You should put the brain back into the body.

    d) You should take out the eyes.

    e) You can add jewels at the end.

3. The title says. 'Don't read this unless you have a strong stomach!' Why does it say this? Find examples from the text to back up your answer.

Investigations

A **verb** tells us what someone or something is doing, feeling or thinking.

e.g. I *cycle* to school.	→	doing
I *worry* about the tests.	→	feeling
I *think* Maths is difficult.	→	thinking

1. Look at the following sentences about D.I.Y. Mummy and fill in the missing verbs from the list in the box.

   a) This text _____ us how to make a mummy.

   b) The writer _____ a lot of detail.

   c) There are pictures to _____ the text clear.

   d) Some of the instructions _____ quite disgusting.

   e) Others _____ quite funny.

uses	**are**	**tells**	**make**	**sound**

2. The text is made up of a list of instructions. They tell us how to make a mummy. The text is written in imperatives.

   a) On your copy of the text, underline all the imperatives.

      e.g. <u>Take 1 dead body.</u>

   b) Now circle the verb in each imperative.

      e.g. <u>(Take) 1 dead body.</u>

   c) Now complete the following rule about imperatives:

   The verb often comes at the _____ of an imperative.

Help

There are four types of sentence.

• **Statements tell us something:**
'There must be nothing left inside the body.'

• **Questions ask us something:**
'Could this be the origin of an old saying?'

• **Exclamations show surprise or anger or give added emphasis:**
'Don't read this unless you have a strong stomach!'

• **Imperatives tell us to do something:**
'Take 1 dead body.'

Response

Choose one of the following activities to write about:

How to tame a crocodile.

How to become a famous footballer in two weeks.

How to prepare for a new baby in the home.

How to open a carton of milk in the dark, with only a hand-held torch for light.

Now write a set of instructions explaining your activity.

Check!

Remember to use imperatives when writing your instructions.

A3 Harry Potter and the Philosopher's Stone

Harry Potter has been living with his aunt, uncle and cousin, the horrible Dursleys. One night, Harry discovers that he is really a wizard and that he is to go to Hogwarts School of Witchcraft and Wizardry. Harry arrives at the station to catch the train to Hogwarts from Platform $9\frac{3}{4}$. But he begins to worry when he can't find the platform. Then he sees a family who are also going to Hogwarts.

Word Bank

jostled: pushed

'Excuse me,' Harry said to the plump woman.

'Hullo, dear,' she said. 'First time at Hogwarts? Ron's new, too.'

She pointed at the last and youngest of her sons. He was tall, thin and gangling, with freckles, big hands and feet and a long nose.

'Yes,' said Harry. 'The thing is – the thing is, I don't know how to –'

'How to get on to the platform?' she said kindly, and Harry nodded.

'Not to worry,' she said. 'All you have to do is walk straight at the barrier between platforms nine and ten. Don't stop and don't be scared you'll crash into it, that's very important. Best do it at a bit of a run if you're nervous. Go on, go now before Ron.'

'Er – OK,' said Harry.

He pushed his trolley round and stared at the barrier. It looked very solid.

He started to walk towards it. People jostled him on their way to platforms nine and ten. Harry walked more quickly. He was going to smash right into that ticket box and then he'd be in trouble – leaning forward on his trolley he broke into a heavy run – the barrier was coming nearer and nearer – he wouldn't be able to stop – the trolley was out of control – he was a foot away – he closed his eyes ready for the crash –

It didn't come ... he kept on running ... he opened his eyes.

A scarlet steam engine was waiting next to a platform packed with people. A sign overhead said *Hogwarts Express, 11 o'clock*. Harry looked behind him and saw a wrought iron archway where the ticket box had been, with the words *Platform Nine and Three Quarters* on it. He had done it.

Questions

1. Read the passage again. Then answer these questions.

   a) Who is Ron?

   b) Why is the platform called *Platform Nine and Three Quarters*?

   c) How do you get on to the platform?

   d) Why is it best to 'do it at a bit of a run'?

2. In pairs, note down any words in the story which show that:

   a) the woman on the platform is friendly

   b) Harry is nervous

   c) Harry thinks he will crash into the ticket box

   d) the station is busy.

3. How do you think Harry felt when he opened his eyes? Why?

Investigations

1. Look at the following extract from the passage. Which words are actually spoken?

   'Yes,' said Harry. 'The thing is – the thing is, I don't know how to –'
   'How to get on to the platform?' she said kindly, and Harry nodded.

When a writer writes the words that are actually spoken it is called **direct speech**.

2. Match the labels to the correct space to find out the rules for the **punctuation** of direct speech. Write the letter of the correct label in the space provided.

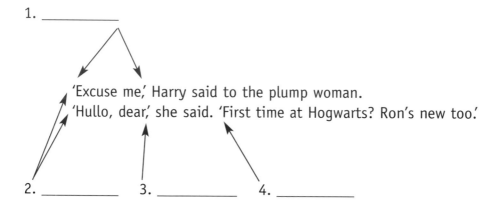

1. _____

'Excuse me,' Harry said to the plump woman.
'Hullo, dear,' she said. 'First time at Hogwarts? Ron's new too.'

2. _____   3. _____   4. _____

Labels

a) A new speaker always starts on a new line.

b) The punctuation goes inside the speech marks.

c) Direct speech begins with a capital letter.

d) The speech marks go around the words that are spoken.

3. Here is a passage taken from *Harry Potter and the Philosopher's Stone* just before the extract on page 16. The speech marks and capital letters have been taken out.

    Rewrite the passage, putting speech marks around the direct speech. Remember to use capital letters for each proper noun (see page 10) and at the start of a new sentence or piece of direct speech. Also remember that a new speaker always starts on a new line.

    > fred, you next, the plump woman said. i'm not fred, i'm george, said the boy. honestly, woman, call yourself our mother? can't you *tell* i'm george? sorry george, dear. only joking, I am fred, said the boy, and off he went.

Response

Everything is different in the world of wizards. The first time Harry does something it is always scary and exciting.

Choose one of the following situations. Then write a short passage showing how Harry finds out what to do and what happens when he does it. Use the plan below to help you.

*   ride a broomstick

    (e.g. has to whisper magic words)

*   make himself invisible

    (e.g. has to wear a magic cloak)

*   see into the future

    (e.g. has to look into a crystal ball)

Plan

Part 1 Explain what Harry must learn to do

Part 2 Harry asks someone to help him

Part 3 The person tells Harry what to do

Part 4 Harry tries it for the first time

Check!

Make sure you follow the rules for writing direct speech when you write down the words that are actually spoken.

A4 Drama Lesson

Working as a class, read the poem _Drama Lesson_. Do you like acting? Or do you prefer to watch drama? What kind of drama do you like to watch on TV or in films?

Drama Lesson

'Let's see some super shapes you blue group,'
Mr Lavender shouts down the hall;
'And forests don't forget your trembly leaves
And stand up straight and tall.'

5 But I've got Phillip Chubb in our group
And he wants to be Robin Hood,
And Ann Boots' sulking 'cos she's not with her friend
And I don't see why I should be wood.

The lights are switched on in the classrooms
10 Outside the sky's nearly black
And the dining hall smells of gravy and cabbage
And Phillip Chubb has boils down his back.

Sir tells Chubb that's he's got to be tree,
But he won't wave his arms around;
15 He says, 'How can I wave me branches, sir,
When someone has chopped them all down?'

Then I come galloping through Sherwood
Following my destiny
And I really believe I'm Robin Hood
20 Come to set Maid Marion free.

At my back I feel my long bow,
My broad sword clanks at my side,
My outlaws gallop close behind
As into adventure we ride.

25 'Untie that maid you villain,' I shout,
With all the strength I have,
But the tree has got bored and is picking his nose
And Maid Marion has gone to the lav.

After rehearsals, Sir calls us together
30 And each group performs its play
But just as it comes to our turn
The bell goes for the end of the day.

As I trudge my way home through the suburbs
The cars and the houses retreat
35 And the thunder of hooves beats in my mind
As I gallop through acres of wheat.

The castle gleams white in the distance
Her banner flaps golden and red
And unheard trumpets weave silver dreams
40 In the landscapes of my head.

Gareth Owen

Questions

1. Answer these questions about the poem.

   a) Who is Mr Lavender? How do you know?

   b) What lines tell you about Phillip Chubb? What kind of person is he?

   c) Look at verse three. How does the speaker feel? Explain your answer.

   d) Now look at verses six and seven. How does the speaker feel now?
      Which words tell you how he is feeling?

2. Find words and phrases in the poem that show that:

   a) at first the speaker finds it hard to enjoy the drama lesson.

   b) later in the lesson, the speaker enjoys the drama.

   c) other students in the class do not enjoy the drama.

   d) on the way home, the speaker thinks about the drama again.

3. Which of the statements below do you think is right? Write down the lines in the
   poem that make you think this.

   a) The speaker finds it easy to imagine different worlds and enjoys doing so.

   b) The speaker does not find it easy to imagine different worlds but enjoys
      doing so.

Investigations

Work with a partner. One of you should work on the first investigation (1 below) and
the other should work on the second investigation (2 below). When you have finished,
share and compare your findings.

1. The poem tells a short story about what happened during and after a drama lesson.
   Your job is to investigate what happened. Write an account of the main events in
   the poem. There are some starting points at the top of the next page.

At the beginning of the lesson, Mr Lavender _____

However, Phillip Chubb _____ and Ann Boots _____

After the group was sorted out _____ .

The speaker wanted to _____ but Phillip and Ann _____

_____

At the end of the lesson _____

As the speaker walked home _____

2. The poem tells us what was going on inside the speaker's head during and after a drama lesson. Your job is to investigate the speaker's thoughts and feelings. Write an account of the speaker's thoughts and feelings. Here are some starting points:

At the beginning of the lesson, the speaker was feeling _____

I know this because _____

When the group started to act, the speaker felt _____
and thought that _____

I know this because _____

At the end of the day, the speaker must have felt _____ ,
but then he imagined _____

Response

Working in your groups, prepare a performance of the poem. As you prepare, think about:

- the different voices in the poem - how will you show these?

- the different sounds in the poem - how will you show these?

- the points in the poem where you need to change your pace or tone to show the difference between what's happening and what the speaker is feeling.

A5 Moving Pictures

This extract explains how moving pictures were first created. As you read, look at the pictures and think about how they help you to understand the information.

1 Moving pictures fascinated many inventors in the nineteenth century.

2 As film-making and photography developed, illustrators and cartoonists began to realise their importance. With moving film they would be able to bring pictures and characters to life!

3 Emile Cohl, a French illustrator, made the first cartoon film in 1908. It was called *Fantasmagorie* and lasted for only two minutes. In the USA, comic strip artist Winsor McCay used his simple style of drawing to make cartoon films such as *Gertie the Dinosaur* (1909). His work was an immediate success.

4 To make cartoon films, a series of still pictures flash before the audience's eyes so quickly that the images appear to be moving. A cartoon film is actually made up of thousands of pictures.

5 In the early days of cartoon films, illustrators had to draw every single movement in a new picture. All the pictures were then photographed (shot) one after another, on to a reel of film. Drawing the pictures took a long time. That is why the comic strip style of cartoons developed. The simpler the style of drawing, as in cartoon pictures, the easier it was to make large numbers of pictures.

6 The heavy workload of the illustrators was changed by the introduction of 'cel' animation. The drawings were put on clear sheets of film, called celluloid. One image could be put on top of another.

7 This meant that fewer drawings were needed. For example, if a dog wagged its tail, one drawing of the main body of the dog could be made. Separate drawings on celluloid, of the tail moving, would be laid over the picture of the rest of the dog. In this way the whole dog would not have to be redrawn for each movement.

Questions

1. Choose the correct answer to complete these sentences.

   a) The first cartoon film

   i)   was made in 1908.

   ii) was called *Gertie the Dinosaur.*

   iii) was made by Winsor McCay.

   b) In the early days of cartoon films

   i)   illustrators used 'cel' animation.

   ii) illustrators had to draw every movement in a new picture.

   iii) it was easy to make a large number of pictures.

   c) 'Cel' animation means

   i)   changing the heavy workload of illustrators.

   ii) drawings are put on clear film on top of each other.

   iii) a picture of a dog wagging its tail.

2. Look at the pictures in the passage and answer the questions below.

   a) Look at the picture of Gertie. What sort of character do you think she was? Was she fierce, dangerous or friendly? Explain your answer.

   b) Do the pictures help to make the passage easier to understand? Why or why not?

3. If you were the writer of this passage, would you have used any more pictures? If so, what would they show?

Investigations

1. Look at the passage again. It is written in seven **paragraphs**. These are numbered for you. In pairs, decide what is the main topic of each paragraph. Write one sentence for each one.

   e.g.   Paragraph 1   Inventors were interested in moving pictures in the nineteenth century.

2. Look at the beginning of each paragraph. How does each paragraph link to the one before it? Use the following starting points to help you.

e.g.   Paragraph 1 is about the early days of moving pictures.

Paragraph 2 begins 'As film-making and photography developed...' This continues the explanation of how moving pictures started.

Paragraph 3 begins 'Emile Cohl, a French illustrator, made the first cartoon film in 1908.' This continues _____

Paragraph 4 begins 'To make cartoon films...'
This continues _____

Paragraph 5 begins 'In the early days of cartoon films...'
This continues _____

Paragraph 6 begins _____

Paragraph 7 _____

Response

Work with a partner. You and your partner are going to give a short talk about a film that you have both enjoyed or found interesting. Decide which film you are going to talk about. Then prepare your talk by making notes under the following headings. These are your main topics.

*   THE PLOT
    What happened in the film?

*   YOUR FAVOURITE CHARACTER
    Who was he or she? Why did you like him or her?

*   SPECIAL EFFECTS
    Were there any special effects that made the film memorable?

*   RECOMMENDATION
    Why do you think other people in your class would enjoy this film?

When you have prepared your notes, give your talk to the rest of your class or your group.

Check!

Remember to link each paragraph together.

Test Yourself!

In this section, you have learnt about:
- nouns
- sentences
- verbs
- punctuating direct speech
- using paragraphs.

Answer the following questions to check you have understood what you have learnt.

1. Fill in the gaps in the following passage with nouns from the box below. Remember to use a capital letter for a proper noun.

   _____a)_____ writes jokes and silly _____b)_____ .

   He writes for _____c)_____ .

   _____d)_____ writes for children and _____e)_____ .

   He lives in _____f)_____ .

   He has won lots of _____g)_____ .

stories	children	prizes	david almond	michael rosen	adults	norfolk

2. a) Underline the verbs in the following sentences.

   i) Cut the body.

   ii) Take out the intestines.

   iii) Clean the insides.

   iv) Fill it with spices.

   b) What kind of sentences are these?

3. Complete the following rules for writing direct speech.

   a) Put speech marks _____ the words that are spoken.

   b) Put the punctuation _____ the speech marks.

   c) Start the speech with _____ .

   d) Put each speaker on a new _____ .

Section B
Naughty to Nasty

Some of the pieces of writing in this section are about naughty people. And some are about downright nasty people.

In this section, you will learn about:

- rhyme and rhythm
- adjectives
- how to understand character
- identifying fact and opinion
- the layout of leaflets.

B1 Growing Up

This poem is about growing up.
Read the poem aloud.

Word Bank

clout: hit

Growing up

I know a lad called Billy
Who goes along with me
He plays this game
Where he uses my name
And makes people think that he's me.

Don't ever mess with Billy
He's a vicious sort of bloke
He'll give you a clout
For saying nowt
And thump you for a joke.

My family can't stand Billy
Can't bear him around the place
He won't eat his food
He's always rude
And wears scowls all over his face.

No one can ever break Billy
He's got this look in his eye
That seems to say
You can whale me all day
But you'll not make Billy cry.

He has a crazy face has Billy
Eyes that look but can't see
A mouth like a latch
Ears that don't match
And a space where his brains should be.

Mad Billy left one morning
Crept away without being seen
Left his body for me
That fits perfectly
And a calm where his madness had been.

Gareth Owen

Questions

1. Read to the end of the poem and answer these questions.

   a) Who did you think Billy was at the beginning of the poem?

   b) Who do you think Billy is at the end of the poem?

   c) What are three of the bad things that Billy does?

   d) How do you know that Billy will not do these things again?

   e) Where has Billy gone?

2. Which of these words best describes the speaker? Explain your choice.

naughty	clever	violent	thoughtful

3. Which of the following statements do you agree with? Find words and phrases from the passage to explain your choice.

   This poem is about the fact that young people act without thinking.

   This poem is about the changes that happen to you as you grow up.

Investigations

Answer the following questions about the poem.

    a) How many times does the word 'Billy' appear?

    b) Where does the word 'Billy' appear in each line?

    c) Why do you think the position changes in the last verse?

Rhyme

1. Sometimes poets use rhyme to make words stand out. There are many rhyming pairs in this poem. Match the word in column A with its rhyming pair in column B.

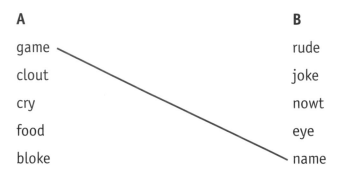

A	B
game	rude
clout	joke
cry	nowt
food	eye
bloke	name

2. Read the made-up stanza below. This stanza does not rhyme.

> **I know a lad called Billy**
> **I go round with him all the time**
> **He plays this game**
> **And calls himself Billy**
> **So that people think he's me**

Do you like this stanza more or less than the others? Why or why not?

Rhythm

Poems are written in lines. Each line has a number of beats. This is called rhythm.

The beats in the stanza below have been printed in bold.

> Don't **ev**er **mess** with **Bill**y
>
> He's a **vic**ious **sort** of **bloke**
>
> He'll **give** you a **clout**
>
> For **say**ing **nowt**
>
> And **thump** you **for** a **joke**

Read the stanza aloud, clapping on the beats.

Find the beats in the rest of the poem by reading it aloud, clapping at the same time.

 Response

Write your own poem about yourself.

- First think of the kind of person you have been in the past.

  Are you pleased with how you have acted?

  What was good or bad about you?

  Have you changed at all? How?

- Then write your poem in the same style as the one on page 30.

Each stanza has five lines

The first line always ends with your name

Lines 2 and 5 rhyme

Lines 3 and 4 rhyme

The final verse changes and the name appears at the beginning of the first line.

B2 Gollum

This is a description of a strange creature called Gollum. It comes from the book *The Hobbit*.

Word Bank

throttled: strangled

Deep down here by the dark water lived old Gollum, a small slimy creature. I don't know where he came from, nor who or what he was. He was Gollum – as dark as darkness, except for two big round pale eyes in his thin face. He had a little boat, and he rowed about quite quietly on the lake; for lake it was, wide and deep and deadly cold. He paddled it with large feet dangling over the side, but never a ripple did he make. Not he. He was looking out of his pale lamp-like eyes for blind fish, which he grabbed with his long fingers as quick as thinking. He liked meat too. Goblin he thought good, when he could get it; but he took care they never found him out. He just throttled them from behind, if they ever came down alone anywhere near the edge of the water, while he was prowling about.

Questions

1. Decide whether the following statements about Gollum are true or false. If a sentence is false, write down the truth.

   a) Gollum lives under water.

   b) Gollum rows his boat on the lake.

   c) Gollum has large feet.

   d) Gollum has big dark eyes.

   e) Gollum doesn't like meat.

2. Find the words and phrases in the passage which show:

   a) Gollum is mysterious

   b) the lake is large

   c) Gollum is careful when killing.

3. What do each of the following phrases mean?

   a) as dark as darkness

   b) as quick as thinking

   c) Goblin he thought good.

Investigations

An **adjective** is a word that describes a noun.

> e.g. He had a **little** boat.
>
> He grabbed with his **long** fingers.

An adjective can be before the noun.

> e.g. He was a **small slimy** creature.

An adjective can also be after the noun

> e.g. The lake was **wide**.

1. Look at the chart below.

   a) There are some nouns from the passage in the first column. Find those nouns in the passage.

   b) Now find the adjectives that describe each noun. Write the adjectives in the second column, next to the noun they describe. Some nouns have more than one adjective.

Noun	Adjective
water	_____
eyes (1)	1 _____ 2 _____ 3 _____ 4 _____
face	_____
lake	1 _____ 2 _____ 3 _____
eyes (2)	1 _____ 2 _____
fish	_____

2. Adjectives are sometimes used to give a certain feeling or atmosphere to a passage. Look at the adjectives you wrote down in the chart. What impression of Gollum do the adjectives give you? Choose one of the following words.

evil	mysterious	dangerous	sad	angry

Response

Look at the following drawing. It shows a strange creature who lives in the desert. You are going to write a description of this creature.

1. First decide whether you think this creature is friendly or dangerous. When you have decided, think of the adjectives you could use to describe him to create the feeling you want.

	Friendly	**Dangerous**
e.g.	warm	sharp
	round	long
	soft	strong

2. When you have made your list, write your description using the adjectives you have chosen. You should include the following points in your description.

    a) What the creature looks like

    b) How the creature moves

    c) What the creature eats and how he find his food.

B3 The Fwog Prince

Read or listen to the following play being read. It is a different version of the fairy tale *The Frog Prince*. In this version, things are rather different to the original.

Scene 1: That fateful morning

(NARRATOR, FX, FAIRYTALE VOICE, PRINCE, MONA, KING P, GROVEL, McNORTY)

NARRATOR   You've probably heard the story of the Frog Prince. You know – spoilt Princess drops golden ball into a well. A talking frog appears and fetches the ball. The frog turns out to be a handsome Prince. Then they get married.

       . . . Have you ever wondered about all this? Doesn't it all seem rather unlikely? I think it's time somebody told the truth. But be warned. There is nobody nice in this story at all . . .

FX   SOFT COURTLY MUSIC.

FAIRYTALE VOICE   Once upon a time there was a handsome Prince who had the misfortune to offend a Witch. In revenge, the Witch cast a spell over the Prince.

NARRATOR   Well, now, let's get the facts straight. Prince Pipsqueak was *not* handsome. Oh, he was a Prince all right. He had the castle with attached moat, crown, horse, coach, servants, smart clothes, expensive shoes, but take all that away and he was quite ordinary. Except – when he opened his mouth.

PRINCE   I say! Peasant! Thwow down your cloak. I wish to cwoss over this puddle!

NARRATOR   When he did that, he used a Certain Tone of Voice.

PRINCE   You there! Waiter! This cup is cwacked. Don't you know I'm the Pwince?

NARRATOR   So it's time to tell you what *really* happened on that fateful morning. Prince Pipsqueak woke as usual.

PRINCE   Wun my bath. Squeeze my toothpaste. Bwush my hair.

GROVEL   Good morning, sir. May I say how handsome you look first thing.

PRINCE   Ah, Gwovel, I want a light bweakfast. Just four kippers, two boiled eggs, four washers of bacon and mounds of toast and marmalade, served on my golden tway.

> ## Word Bank
>
> FX: sound effect
> monogwammed: something that is monogrammed
> has the owner's initials on it

GROVEL　　At once, sir. Lovely day, sir. Nice day for a dip I'd say.

PRINCE　　Smart thinking, Gwovel. I shall take a wefweshing dip in the moat and pwactise my bwest stwoke. I want my costume, my goggles, my flippers and my monogwammed wubber wing, and be quick! I'm the Pwince you know.

NARRATOR　While Pipsqueak was getting ready, the Witch was already up. Old Mrs McNorty lived in a tumbledown hut in the castle grounds. In fact, she had retired from witchcraft. There wasn't the call for it these days. So she'd got a job keeping the moat free of leaves. She hardly ever bothered with magic any more. Except at full moon, of course. Full moon always made her corns play up – and when Mrs McNorty's corns were playing up, she was *wicked*. As it happened, there had been a full moon the night before.

McNORTY　My corns are killing me.

NARRATOR　And as there was no one around, Mrs McNorty sat down at the edge of the moat, removed her boots, and lowered her poor old throbbing feet into the cold water.

McNORTY　Ah.

NARRATOR　Just at that moment, Prince Pipsqueak appeared. It was then that Pipsqueak made his terrible mistake. He used that Certain Tone of Voice.

PRINCE　　I say there! Old woman! Stop that at once!

McNORTY　Are you talking to me, Sonny?

PRINCE　　I most certainly am! You're dirtying my water!

McNORTY　I'll give you dirt. The cheek of it!

PRINCE　　Now listen here. If you don't take your disgusting feet out of my moat immediately, I shall have you awwested. *I* am the Pwince.

McNORTY　Not any more you're not.

FX　　　　A PUFF OF SMOKE. THE 'RIBBIT, RIBBIT' OF A FROG.

NARRATOR　It was as simple as that. One moment Pipsqueak was a Prince. A small green puff of smoke later, he was a frog.

Questions

1. Answer the following questions.

    a) What warning does the narrator give at the start of the play?

    b) What does the word 'grovel' mean?
        Why is this a good name for the Prince's servant?

    c) What was Mrs McNorty doing when she met the Prince?

    d) Why did Mrs McNorty turn the Prince into a frog?

2. Complete the sentences below. Use the words in the box to help you.

impatient	naughty	spoilt	angry	bossy	bad-tempered

    a) I think the Prince is _____ because _____

    b) I think Mrs McNorty is _____ because _____

3. Write down what you think happens next. Use these questions to help you to plan:

    Where will the Fwog Prince go?

    Who will he meet?

    How will he explain who he is?

    Will they believe him?

Investigations

You can find out more about a character in a text by looking at:

*   how he or she speaks

*   what he or she does.

Work through the following activities to find out more about the **character** of the Prince. Work on a copy of the text.

How the Prince speaks

1. The Prince cannot pronounce the letter 'r'. Instead he says 'w'.

   a) Use one colour to underline all the words where the letter 'w' is used for the sound 'r'. In the margin, write the correct spelling.

   e.g.   PRINCE   <u>Thwow</u> down your cloak   Throw

   b) The Prince is very bossy. He likes telling people what to do. Sometimes he shouts when he gives an order. This is often shown by an exclamation mark (!). Use a second colour to mark all the lines that the Prince might shout.

   c) Now try reading aloud the words spoken by the Prince. As you read, notice the parts that you have underlined. What do these words and lines tell you about the character of the Prince?

What the Prince does

2. Look at each line spoken by the Prince and next to it write a word that describes his behaviour.

   e.g.   PRINCE   I say! Peasant! Thwow down your cloak!   Bossy
                   I wish to cwoss over this puddle!

Response

Work in groups of three. Decide who will read the following parts:

- Prince
- Narrator/Grovel
- Fairytale Voice/McNorty

a) Practise reading your own lines to yourself. Ask someone in your group to help you with any difficult words. Try dividing long words into syllables.
   e.g. ex/pen/sive = expensive

b) Now read the playscript in your groups. Practise several times.

c) Perform your reading to the rest of the class. Ask them to suggest how you could improve it.

B4 Phoolan Devi

This piece of writing tells you about the life of Phoolan Devi. She was a bandit leader in India and was called 'The Beautiful Robber'. Read the text to find out about her extraordinary life.

Phoolan Devi

Phoolan Devi was born in a poor village in northern India. She had two sisters, but her father always singled her out for punishment and hard work. When she was only eleven years old, he arranged that she should be married to a much older man.

In her new home, Phoolan Devi was treated as a slave. She ran away and began a wretched time of wandering and begging for food. In despair,

ravine:	a deep narrow gorge or valley
patrol:	a group of policemen searching for bandits
markswoman:	a woman who is good at hitting targets with a gun
vengeance:	revenge
massacre:	murder of a number of people

she fell in with a band of dacoits (the Indian word for bandits). She joined them on their expeditions, robbing, looting and kidnapping prisoners for ransom.

Phoolan Devi found this way of life much more enjoyable. She learned how to shoot a rifle, how to hide in the maze of nearby ravines and how to avoid patrols. Her teacher was Vikram Mallah, the leader of the gang.

The dacoits often fought amongst themselves. One day in 1980 Vikram was shot dead by two rivals, the Singh brothers. They seized Phoolan Devi and carried her away. For three weeks they beat her and abused her. Then she escaped, swearing to have her revenge.

Phoolan Devi joined another gang. It wasn't long before she became its leader. She was brave, ruthless and a fine markswoman. Besides this, she seemed to be able to escape from any police trap. Throughout northern India, she became famous as 'The Beautiful Robber'.

She still wanted vengeance on the Singh brothers. In February, 1981, her dacoit band surrounded the village of Behmai, where the Singh family lived. The brothers could not be found; even so Devi's dacoits killed twenty-four of their relatives and friends.

The massacre caused a storm of horror. Thousands of policemen combed the hills for Phoolan Devi. But for two more years she escaped them. Finally, exhausted and ill, she gave herself up. In exchange for her surrender, she was not executed, but put in jail. She is still there today.

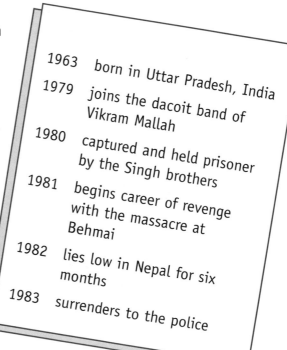

1963   born in Uttar Pradesh, India

1979   joins the dacoit band of Vikram Mallah

1980   captured and held prisoner by the Singh brothers

1981   begins career of revenge with the massacre at Behmai

1982   lies low in Nepal for six months

1983   surrenders to the police

Questions

1. Choose the correct answer to complete the following sentences.

   a) The first paragraph tells us that:

      i) Phoolan Devi was small for her age

      ii) Phoolan Devi's father picked on her

      iii) Phoolan Devi was unhappy

      iv) Phoolan Devi never went to school.

   b) Phoolan Devi ran away because:

      i) she wanted to join the dacoits

      ii) she had to beg for food

      iii) she had a new home

      iv) she was treated as a slave.

   c) Phoolan Devi gave herself up to the police because:

      i) she had escaped for two years

      ii) she was tired and sick

      iii) she was not executed

      iv) she is in jail.

2. Read the following sentences. They are all about the passage you have just read, but they are in the wrong order. Put the sentences in the right order.

   a) Phoolan Devi joined a band of dacoits.

   b) In 1981, the dacoit band killed 24 people.

   c) Phoolan Devi gave herself up to the police.

   d) Vikram was shot dead by the Singh brothers.

   e) Phoolan Devi was born in a village in northern India.

   f) She ran away from home.

3. The capture of Phoolan Devi is going to be on the radio. Write the news flash telling people about it. Write at least six sentences. Put in all the information listeners will want to hear. You may like to start like this:

   > News flash!
   >
   > Today Phoolan Devi gave herself up to the police...

Investigations

A **fact** is something that is true.

> e.g. **Phoolan Devi was born in northern India.**

An **opinion** is somebody's point of view.

> e.g. **Phoolan Devi was a bad woman.**

1. Read the sentences below. Which are facts and which are opinions?

    a) She learned how to shoot a rifle.

    b) She was brave and ruthless.

    c) The Singh family lived in the village of Behmai.

    d) She is still in jail today.

    e) Phoolan Devi is very beautiful.

2. Find four more facts about Phoolan Devi and write them down.

3. Now write down one sentence giving your own opinion of Phoolan Devi.

Response

> **Phoolan Devi was a bad and cruel woman.**

Write whether you agree with this or not. In your writing you should give your opinion. You could use the following frame to help you. Write about 50 words.

I think that Phoolan Devi was/was not a bad and cruel woman.

I think this because _____ .

She did this because _____ .

It is my opinion that she is _____ .

B5 Stop Them Taking Your Bike for a Ride

Word Bank

opportunist thief: a thief who steals if there is an easy opportunity, such as an open door, or an unlocked bike

deterrent: something that stops someone doing something

Have you ever had anything stolen? What was it? Was it ever returned? The police produce a number of helpful booklets to try to help people to prevent theft. This is part of one booklet about preventing bike theft.

In 1996 the National Cycling Strategy was launched in the UK. The aim of this strategy is to encourage the wider use of bicycles by making cycling easier, safer and more convenient. 150,000 bicycles are stolen every year, and many are never recovered. But bicycle theft is preventable, and this booklet suggests ways in which you can protect your property.

LOCKS AND BOLTS

There are many different products on the market and price is not the only indicator of quality. **Also important is how long the product resisted attack.**

You should look for products that have been tested against attack. Look on the packaging and also ask your retailer for advice.

- To guard against the **opportunist** thief you need a product that has resisted attack for **one minute**.

- To guard against the **determined** thief you need a product that has resisted attack for **three minutes**.

- To guard against the **dedicated** thief you need a product that has resisted attack for **five minutes**.

Stop them taking your bike for a ride

PROPERTY MARKING

Marking your bike can act as a **deterrent** to theft and may also help the police to return it to you if it is stolen and then recovered.

To be effective, a security marking must:

(i) **be clearly visible**. Hidden marks do not deter theft unless they are backed up by visible ones – a tamper proof label for instance;

(ii) **be securely fixed**. If it comes off easily and leaves no trace then it won't deter a thief;

(iii) **be placed in two separate locations** on the bicycle and not on any part which is readily removable or replaceable;

(iv) **give clear information** that will quickly lead the finder to the owner of the bicycle.

Questions

1. What is the aim of the National Cycling Strategy?

2. Which of the sentences below are true and which are false? If a sentence is false, write down what the truth is.

    a) Most people who have their bike stolen get their bike back.

    b) An expensive product is usually the best quality.

    c) You should buy products that have been tested.

    d) You should put a security mark in more than one place.

3. Look at the section called 'Property Marking'.

    a) Write down the four main points about effective property marking in this section.

    b) How did you find these points?

Investigations

Layout

1. Look at the following outline of one of the pages. Below is a list of presentational features. Match each presentational feature to the correct part of the text.

    a) Use of bullet points

    b) Use of sub-headings

    c) Use of bold text

    d) Use of imperative sentence ? (see page 15)

> In 1990 the National Cycling Strategy was launched in the UK. The aim of this strategy is to encourage the wider use of bicycles by making cycling easier, safer and more convenient. 150,000 bicycles are stolen every year, and many are never recovered. But bicycle theft is preventable, and this booklet suggests ways in which you can protect your property.
>
> **1** → **LOCKS AND BOLTS**
>
> There are many different products on the market and price is not the only indicator of quality. **Also important is how long the product resisted attack.**
>
> **2** → You should look for products that have been tested against attack. Look on the packaging and also ask your retailer for advice.
>
> **3** →
> - To guard against the **opportunist** thief you need a product that has resisted attack for **one minute**.
>
> **4** →
> - To guard against the **determined** thief you need a product that has resisted attack for **three minutes**.
> - To guard against the **dedicated** thief you need a product that has resisted attack for **five minutes**.

2. Now match these two parts of a sentence to explain why each presentational feature is used. This first one has been done for you.

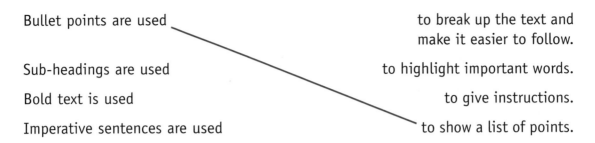

Bullet points are used   to break up the text and make it easier to follow.

Sub-headings are used   to highlight important words.

Bold text is used   to give instructions.

Imperative sentences are used   to show a list of points.

Response

The booklet about bike theft was written for adults. However, many young children also own bikes and need to know how to take care of them. Choose one part of the booklet to rewrite for young children. Follow the steps below to help you.

1. Look carefully at the language of the section you have chosen. Are there any difficult words or phrases?

    e.g. **Marking your bike can act as a <u>deterrent</u>...**

2. Use a dictionary to find out the meaning of the difficult words and choose simpler words or phrases to replace them.

    e.g. **Marking your bike can stop thieves stealing it.**

3. Look at the sentences in the section you have chosen. Are there any long or complicated sentences?

    e.g. **There are many different products on the market and price is not the only indicator of quality.**

4. Rewrite these sentences in a simpler way.

    e.g. **There are many different products. The most expensive are not always the best.**

5. Illustrate your page to make the meaning clearer for a young child.

Test Yourself!

In this section, you have learnt about:
- **rhyme and rhythm**
- **adjectives**
- **how to understand character**
- **identifying fact and opinion**
- **the layout of leaflets.**

Answer the following questions to check you have understood what you have learnt.

1. Copy out the following stanza.

    a) Put a circle around the words that rhyme.

    b) Underline the beats in the lines.

    > I know a lad called Billy
    >
    > We play a funny game
    >
    > He says he's me
    >
    > And sets me free
    >
    > To have a different name.

2. Put the following adjectives into two groups. Group 1 contains adjectives to describe a friendly creature. Group 2 contains adjectives to describe a dangerous creature.

warm	angry	smiling	hard	evil	playful	soft	cold

3. Which of the following sentences are facts and which are opinions?

    a) The information about Phoolan Devi is very interesting.

    b) Phoolan Devi was born in northern India.

    c) She was known as 'The Beautiful Robber'.

    d) The information about her is very clear.

    e) The picture is very helpful.

Entertainment has changed over the years. A long time ago, people used to tell each other stories and tales. These days people play on computers, read magazines, play sport or watch TV. What do you do in your spare time?

Get into the
ACTION

Check out our game
Check out our prices -
We'll not be beaten!

Free starter pack for
SHOOT readers

Call today for your
FREE no obligation
start-up pack

In this section, you will learn about:

- characters
- connectives
- persuading people
- verb tenses
- direct and reported speech.

C1 Roger the Dodger

This extract is from a comic called *The Beano*. In this extract, Roger the Dodger tries to dodge some work on a farm.

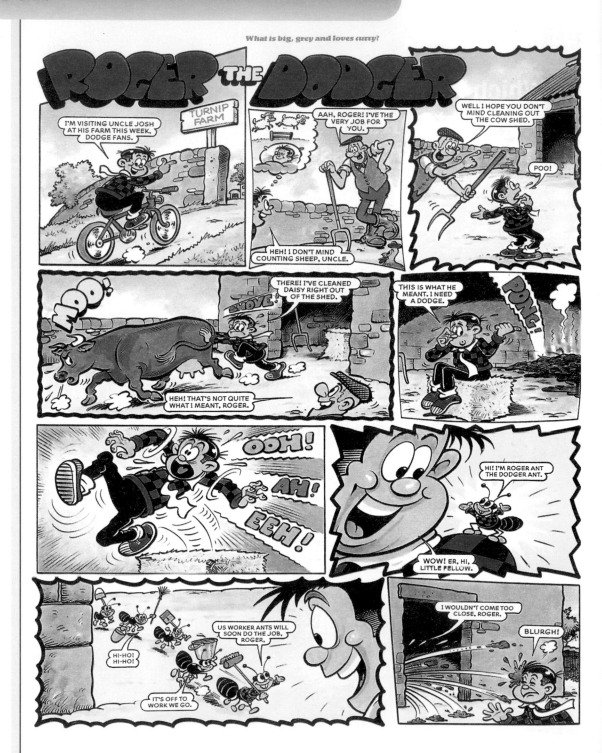

Questions

1. Put the following sentences in the correct order.

   a) Roger's uncle asks him to clean the cow shed.

   b) The ant takes the bull back to the farm.

   c) The bull escapes.

   d) Roger gives the ants some food.

   e) The worker ants clean the shed for Roger.

2. a) Look carefully at the drawings of the ants. Which of the following words do you think best describe the ants?

friendly	lazy	cheerful	unhappy	angry	helpful

   b) How did the drawings help you to choose the words?

3. The following words would not be used in real life. Write down what each one means. The first one has been done for you.

   a) Ho-ho!   Shows that Roger is laughing.

   b) Eek!   _____

   c) Blurgh!   _____

   d) Hee-hee!   _____

 Investigations

Look at the plot chart on the next page for the Roger the Dodger story. Then think of a fairy story. Copy and complete the plot chart, using the details of the fairy story. An example has been done for you.

Roger the Dodger	Fairy Tale: Snow White	Your fairy tale
Characters Roger Uncle Josh	**Characters** Snow White Wicked step-mother Seven dwarfs	**Characters** _____ _____ _____
Setting Turnip Farm	**Setting** Palace Seven dwarfs' home	**Setting** _____ _____
Problem Uncle Josh wants Roger to clean the cow shed	**Problem** Wicked step-mother wants Snow White out of the way	**Problem** _____
Conflict (development of problem) Roger does not want to clean the shed	**Conflict** Step-mother tries to kill Snow White with a poisoned apple	**Conflict** _____
Resolution (how the conflict is sorted out) The ants do the work for Roger. They get some food and Uncle Josh is happy.	**Resolution** The Prince saves Snow White.	**Resolution** _____

What similarities can you see between your story and that of Roger the Dodger?

 # Response

Make the first six frames of a comic strip for the fairy story you used in Investigations. Think about who will be in the first six frames, how they will speak, what they will do and what they look like.

In this newspaper extract, Carol Vorderman talks about what she likes to do in her spare time.

What I Watch

Carol Vorderman, maths wizard of C4's 'Countdown', admits to being a TV addict.

I love TV and if I had the chance I think I would watch it all day. It's just as well that I have so much work that I haven't the time.

I've only one TV, but when I'm at home, it's always on. If it was up to me I would have one in every room in the house, the bathroom as well; but my family won't let me.

If I could watch one programme, then it would be 'Coronation Street'. I love it. And 'Who Wants to be a Millionaire'. One minute you are sitting on the edge of your chair, hardly daring to breathe. Next you are helpless with laughter.

One of my favourite recent programmes is 'Cold Feet' and another is 'The Royle Family'. In different ways they are works of TV genius because they both show what real life is like.

I do watch the news as often as I can, as I don't have time to read the papers. I usually watch 'The Eleven O'Clock News' and 'ITN News at 5.40'.

For something quite different, 'Blind Date' takes some beating. It is so funny. I feel a bit embarrassed when the people in it try to be funny; but most of the time they are just themselves. As for Cilla Black, I don't think anyone else could do it so well. She is everyone's big sister.

Whenever I can, I spend Saturday afternoons with C4 watching black-and-white films from the '30s and '40s. I love the weepy ones, with stars like Bette Davis and Joan Crawford. Or I enjoy re-runs of 'A Touch of Frost' or 'Inspector Morse'.

Questions

1. Read the following questions and choose the right answer.

   a) What does Carol think of TV?

   i) She loves watching TV.

   ii) She thinks people watch too much TV.

   b) Why does she not watch much TV?

   i) She does not watch much TV because there is nothing she likes.

   ii) She does not watch much TV because she is too busy.

   c) Why does Carol like 'Who Wants to be a Millionaire'?

   i) She likes 'Who Wants to be a Millionaire' because it's exciting.

   ii) She likes 'Who Wants to be a Millionaire' because it's like Coronation Street.

2. Answer the following questions.
   a) Why does Carol watch so much news?
   b) How does Carol feel when she watches 'Blind Date'?

3. This article appeared in the *TV Times* – a paper that tells you what is on TV. Why do you think they chose to include this article in that paper?

Investigations

Sometimes a writer will join sentences together to make longer sentences.

> e.g. **I do watch the news as often as I can. I don't have time to read the papers.**
>
> *becomes*
>
> **I do watch the news as often as I can, as I don't have time to read the papers.**

We use **connectives** to join sentences together. Some common connectives are:

and	but	yet	because	or	so	while	when	which	as

1. Read the following sentences and fill in the missing connectives. Use the box at the bottom of page 58 to help you.

    a) Carol can't watch much TV _____ she is too busy.

    b) The TV is always on _____ Carol is at home.

    c) She doesn't really like soaps _____ she watches 'Coronation Street'.

    d) Carol doesn't have time to read the papers _____ she watches the news on TV.

    e) She watches 'The Eleven O'Clock News' _____ she watches 'ITN News at 5.40'.

2. Look at the paragraphs beginning 'I think it is the best programme' to 'ITN News at 5.40'. On your copy of the text, underline all the connectives.

    e.g.   **One of my favourite recent programmes is 'Cold Feet' <u>and</u> another is 'The Royle Family'.**

3. Rewrite the paragraphs you looked at in Investigations 2, taking out the connectives. You may have to change some of the words.

    e.g.   **One of my favourite recent programmes is 'Cold Feet. Another is 'The Royle Family'.**

4. When you have finished, read your version of the passage. What difference do the short sentences make? Why did the writer use connectives to make longer sentences?

Response

What do you think of TV?

Write a short article saying what you like or dislike about TV. Remember to use connectives to join sentences together where appropriate. Use the following plan to help you:

> **Paragraph 1 – What you think of TV**
>
> **Paragraph 2 – How many TVs you have in your house and how often you watch TV**
>
> **Paragraph 3 – Your favourite TV programme and why you like it**
>
> **Paragraph 4 – Which TV programme you don't like and why**
>
> **Paragraph 5 – Conclusion**

The following two extracts are from *Shoot!* magazine. Read them carefully. Do they make you want to buy the product?

Oi YOU!

HOW DO YOU FANCY SCORING LOADSA GOALS, EARNING PILES OF CASH AND LIFTING THE PREMIERSHIP TROPHY?

uLet Your Boots Do The

Shoot
THE BOARD GAME

SPECIAL MAIL ORDER PRICE OF £19.99 + £3.96 POSTAGE & PACKING

Cheques and postal orders, made out to Grape Distribution Services Ltd, should be sent to: Shoot Board Game, Grape Distribution Services Ltd, 63/64 West Yard, Camden Lock Place, London, NW1 8AF. Telephone orders on 0171-485-2700 — all major credit cards and Switch accepted.

PLAY Shoot THE BOARD GAME AND YOU'LL GET YOUR CHANCE!

Shoot THE BOARD GAME: IT'S JUST LIKE THE REAL THING!

Questions

1. Read the advert for *Extra Time*. Then answer the questions below.

   a) What is the first piece of writing you notice?

   b) What makes that piece of writing stand out? Think about the use of colour and capital letters and the position on the page.

   c) What is unusual about the bullets? Why are they like this?

2. Read the advert for *Shoot*. Discuss how the advert makes the game sound exciting. Start by looking for:

   a) direct address to the reader (use of 'you')

   b) three descriptions of what might happen if you play the game.

3. Who do you think these adverts are for? Why?

Investigations

Advertisements try to **persuade people** to buy something. They use a number of methods to do this. Complete the table by finding examples of the different methods from each advert.

Feature of writing to persuade	Example from *Extra Time*	Example from *Shoot The Board Game*
Imperatives (see page 15)	Check out our game	_____
Details of how to order	Coupon in bottom corner	_____
Exclamation marks	Join now and see why there are thousands of members playing in Extra Time!	_____
Repeating of key words or phrases	Check out our game Check out our prices	_____ _____
Large print or capital letters	Get into the ACTION	_____
Statements that are not complete sentences	Full automated email option	_____
Use of positive adjectives	Uncheatable transfer system	_____

Response

Design your own advertisement for a sports product, such as a new strip or game.

- First decide what you are going to advertise. Write down all the details you must include:

  What is your product?

  What is so good about your product?

  What kind of person will buy your product? (How old are they?)

  How much does your product cost?

  How can people order your product?

- Now think about the language you will use:

  What is the most important thing to say about your product?

  What kind of language do you need to use for the people who might buy your product?

  What adjectives will you use?

  What imperative sentences will you use?

- Finally, decide how you are going to present the advert. Think about using:

  Different colours

  Capital letters

  Pictures

  Different sized text

- You may decide to create the advertisement on a computer. If so, think about using different fonts.

The following words and phrases may help you.

FREE!   While stocks last   *Win*   ENJOY

Be a Star!   Call today   Unique   **Great Value!**

Exciting   WANT TO BE A...?   **Don't miss this...**

For more information...

In this extract, Bazzer has just bought a tamagotcha – an electronic pet. He has called it Tazzer.

As we walked along, Bazzer kept gazing at the Tama and talking to it in a stupid baby way. 'Cootchy cootchy coo', and 'Hello little Tazzer!'

'Long live the People's Republic of China,' the wretched thing kept answering.

It asked for things all the time. I began to think it'd never shut up. 'Tazzer play', 'Tazzer watch telly', 'Tazzer sleep', only each time it didn't finish its words. It sounded even sillier when it wanted a drink – 'Tazzer sup', it said. It was beginning to get on my nerves.

'Can't you turn it down?' I asked. 'Everyone's staring.'

'Keeps you busy, doesn't it,' said Bazzer. 'Who's a naughty little Tazzer, then? Whoops, it needs cleaning again,' he said regretfully.

I knew what he meant. It seemed a lot of money to have spent on something which wanted your attention the whole time and did nothing back except repeat, 'Long live the People's Republic of China'. That made it worse. I began to resent the thing. I thought of the gun symbol and half wished it'd turn the gun on itself. The Tama-pain-in-the-neck, I mean.

Word Bank

gun symbol:	there is a symbol of a gun on the computer screen
commotion:	fuss
rigid:	stiff
intervened:	interrupted
anguish:	pain
simultaneously:	at the same time

We wandered through into some of the back streets to get into the shade and avoid some of the staring people.

Almost immediately I heard something. Shouting and some kind of action. I glanced over the road. There was a bank there, and that's where the commotion was coming from.

At first, I thought they were filming some kind of action scene for a soap or something. Then I realised this was no acting. A young man – not much older than us – came out of the bank waving a gun, and carrying a bag which must've contained money. Exactly like those action dramas you see on the telly.

The bank robber – I'd twigged by then – waved the gun in the air. He looked scared rigid. I understood how he felt. I ducked behind a parked car and watched through the side window. I'm no fool, and catching bullets isn't my favourite pastime. But Bazzer didn't. Well, that's typical of him.

Bazzer said later that he was so excited he just forgot to duck.

Then the Tama Gotcher intervened. 'Long live the People's Republic of China,' it said.

The man with the gun spun round as if we'd shot him in the back. His face was a picture. I could see his point, when you're in the middle of a robbery, it is a bit off-putting to have that called at you.

Bazzer said later it was the man swinging round which scared him most. So much so, he *still* didn't duck and weave.

The Tama Gotcher said, 'Tazzer sup!'

I didn't realise at the time why the man pointed the gun at us. Only later I thought how like 'Hands up!' the Tama's request for a drink must have sounded to an escaping and nervous bank robber.

The robber didn't escape. Instead, he put up his hands. But at that precise moment, when it looked like it was all over, Bazzer must have pressed the wrong button. He swears he pressed the drinks button, but he can't have. It must have been the gun symbol. There was a huge bang as the Tama's gun went off. The Tama gave a cry of anguish, and almost simultaneously Bazzer dropped it. The robber screamed and dropped the gun. If it'd've been me, so would I.

Questions

1. Put the sentences in the correct order.

   a) They went into some back streets.

   b) The bank robber dropped the gun.

   c) A robber ran out of the bank.

   d) The Tama Gotcher said 'Tazzer sup!'

2. Answer these questions:

   a) Why did the speaker want Bazzer to turn Tazzer down?

   b) Why did they go into a back street?

   c) What did the robber think the Tama Gotcher said?

   d) What caused the huge bang?

3. Write a paragraph saying what you think happened next.

Investigations

Read the passage again. The writer has to show things happening at different times. He uses different **verb tenses** to show this.

- We use the present tense to show that something is happening now.

  e.g.   It <u>needs</u> cleaning again.

- We use the past tense to show that something has already happened.

  e.g.   It <u>asked</u> for things all the time.

- We use the future tense to show that something is going to happen.

  e.g.   Bazzer <u>will win</u> a medal.

  He <u>is going to wear it</u> next week.

1. Which tense is each of the following sentences in? The verbs are in bold.

   a) We **wandered** into some back streets.

   b) Everyone **is** staring.

   c) His face **was** a picture.

   d) I **am going to turn** it down.

2. a) Write down a short paragraph about what you did last weekend. Remember to use the past tense. You could start like this.

> Last Saturday, I.......

b) Write down four things about yourself that are true now. Remember to write in full sentences and to use the present tense.

> e.g.   I am sitting in my English class.

c) Write a short paragraph about what you plan to do next weekend. Remember to use the future tense. You could start like this.

> Next Saturday, I am going to.........., After that, I will.......

3. Read the passage from 'We wandered through into some of the back streets' to 'dramas you see on the telly.' Find the verbs in this extract. What tense is it in?

4. Rewrite the passage in the present tense. Start like this:

> We wander through into some of the back streets...

5. Why do you think the writer chose to write in the past tense?

 Response

Look at the following pictures about a robbery.

Write a story based on the pictures.

 Check!

Remember to write in the past tense.

This poem is a ballad. A ballad is a poem that tells a story. This poem tells the story of a girl who is woken up to watch a fire.

My Birthday Treat

I was seven years old at the time.
Yet I remember it all so well
In all my sleeping hours still.
I relive that fiery hell.

Mam woke me with excitement.
The Welsh love all bad news.
She thought it would be a treat for me
To give her fair dues.

'Would you like to see a fire
With engines and police too?
Grandad will watch the others.
I came back for you . . .'

The middle of the night it was.
Sleep stuck blurred my eyes.
A matter of a minute's walk.
Then feel excitement rise.

Many people stood watching.
Just like Guy Fawkes' Night.
I stood with mouth and eyes wide
At such a terrible sight.

Our sawmill's in full flame.
With crackers and Oh's and Ah's.
Eyes like Roman spectators
While moving back their cars.

Then, to my utter terror
A voice shouted, 'Christ, the dogs!'
And I saw my dad disappear
Into the great, burning, crashing logs.

With the true Welsh sense of drama
The mumbling grew to prayers.
It was all right for the others.
It was my dad, not theirs.

I saw him just for a moment.
Black against the glare.
My heart stopped inside me
For he suddenly wasn't there.

'Dad!' I screamed, and met the eyes.
Heard the tuts of gleeful sympathy
Such a lovely spectacle it gave
To see terror in such as me.

I felt my mam's arms about me
Then dad he stood right by.
He yelled, 'Why did you bring her, why?'
All I could do was cry.

I thought of all the horror,
As I still do each night.
Dad was safe next morning.
But my childhood died of fright.

Joan M. Batchelor

Questions

1. The speaker has different feelings in the poem. Write down the words and phrases that show you:

    a) she is excited   b) she is amazed   c) she is frightened

2. What do you think the speaker means in the last line, 'But my childhood died of fright'?

3. Why do you think this poem is in the section of this book called Entertainment? Was it right to put it here?

 ## Investigations

1. How many people speak in this poem?

2. What are the words that are actually spoken? How do you know?

If a writer writes the words that are actually spoken, it is called **direct speech** (see page 18). Sometimes a writer does not use the actual words that are spoken. The writer just describes what is said. This is called **reported speech**.

e.g.   **'Get on the bus,' the bus driver said.**   ➔   direct speech

        The bus driver told us to get on the bus. ➔   reported speech

3. Use these steps to change a sentence in reported speech into direct speech.
    ●   Read the sentence.

        One man shouted that the sawmill was burning.

    ●   What words in the sentence did the man say?

        The sawmill was burning.

    ●   Put speech marks around these words.

        'The sawmill was burning.'

    ●   Write down who was speaking and how they spoke.

 Help

Look at page 18 to remind yourself how to punctuate direct speech.

'The sawmill was burning,' one man shouted.

- Check the punctuation inside the speech brackets.

'The sawmill was burning,' one man shouted.

- Check that the words in direct speech are in the right tense (see pages 66 and 67).

'The sawmill ~~was~~ *is* burning,' one man shouted.

Now change these sentences from reported speech to direct speech.

a) Mam told me to get up.

b) She told me to come and see the fire.

c) My dad said that the dogs were inside.

d) He yelled at us to stand back.

Response

Write the conversation between the speaker's mother and father when they got home after the fire. Before you write your conversation make a few notes under the following headings.

- How does the speaker's father feel about the fire? Is he angry, sad, worried?
- How does the speaker's father feel about his daughter being there? Is he angry, sad, worried?
- How does the speaker's mother feel? Is she pleased she took her daughter or does she regret taking her?
- How will the mother and father speak to each other? Will they be calm or angry? Will they speak quietly or loudly? What will they say?

Use your notes to help you to write the conversation. You could start like this.

When we got home my dad was very angry.

'Why did you take her there?' he asked my mam quietly.

'I thought she should see it,' my mam replied.

Check!

Remember to use direct speech to show the actual words that are spoken.

Test Yourself!

In this section, you have learnt about:
- characters
- connectives
- persuading people
- verb tenses
- direct and reported speech.

Answer the following questions to check you have understood what you have learnt.

1. Join the following pairs of sentences together using a suitable connective.

   a) I like watching TV. I watch it every night.

   b) My favourite programme is 'Top Gear'. I like cars.

   c) I eat my dinner. I watch the news.

   d) I like soaps. I don't watch every episode.

   e) I don't like to watch TV. I have friends at my house.

2. Fill in the blanks with the correct form of the verb in brackets.

   a) Last week, I (get) _____ a new computer.

   b) We (put) _____ it in my bedroom.

   c) I (enjoy) _____ _____ playing computer games.

   d) I (buy) _____ three games yesterday.

   e) Next week, I (buy) _____ a couple more.

3. Change the reported speech into direct speech and the direct speech into reported speech.

   a) 'Some people enjoy watching accidents,' the reporter said.

   b) 'Today there was a fire here in Wales,' he continued.

   c) He explained that a lot of people had come to watch.

   d) He also said that there were even children there.

   e) 'I think it is terrible to bring children to this kind of thing,' he concluded.

Section D
Different Worlds

How do you feel when you go somewhere new and strange, for example, when you start a new school or go to a new place on holiday? Do you feel excited or nervous or both?

In this section, you will learn about:

- adverbs
- alliteration
- similes
- metaphors
- paragraphs
- multiple sentences

Bugsy Malone is a musical play in which children play the parts of gangsters. This extract is the opening scene of the play.

ACT ONE

House lights on.

'BUGSY MALONE' played. Instrumental.

Black. Ominous piano music.

A red light flickers onto the dark stage. **Roxy Robinson** enters along the audience gangway. Scared.

BUGSY (O.S.)   Someone once said, if it was raining brains, Roxy Robinson wouldn't even get wet. In all of New York they didn't come much dumber than Roxy the Weasel. To be frank, Roxy was a dope.

Roxy nervously runs right and left across the stage. Scared. O.S. we hear sound effects: screeching car tyres; slamming car doors; voices.

BRONX CHARLIE (O.S.)   Shoulders, the alley-way quick. He's making for Perito's. Benny cover the back. Yonkers watch the sidewalk.

The **Hoods** enter stage left: **Bronx Charlie, Laughing Boy, Benny Lee,** and **Yonkers. Roxy** is trapped.

The **Hoods** slowly walk towards him. **Roxy** backs away, taking off his hat. Impending disaster. Over this we hear:

BUGSY (O.S.)   Dumb as Roxy was, he could smell trouble like other people could smell gas. But he should never have taken that blind alley by the side of Perito's Bakery.

BRONX CHARLIE   Your name Robinson?

ROXY   Uh huh. (Nods)

BRONX CHARLIE Also known as Roxy the Weasel?

ROXY   Uh huh. (Nods)

BRONX CHARLIE The same Roxy the Weasel who works for Fat Sam?

ROXY   Uh huh. (Nods)

Roxy is splurged and the Hoods walk off. A jump and a click of the heels. Accompanying music.

BUGSY (O.S.) Whatever game it was that everyone was playing, sure as eggs is eggs, Roxy Robinson had been well and truly scrambled.

Two Undertakers walk on and carry off the stiffened body of Roxy, under their arms like a tailor's dummy. A Violinist playing a funeral melody walks behind them.

Light up on Barber cutting Flash Frankie's hair. Radio sound effects of a horse-race. Enter Bugsy stage right.

BUGSY
(to audience) Now, the guy in the chair here is Flash Frankie. The best lawyer in New York. Sure, he's a little shady, but he's the best . . . believe me, Flash Frankie's silver tongue can get a guy out of jail quicker than a truck load of dynamite . . .

The Hoods from previous scene again enter, dramatically. Flash Frankie is splurged, as is the Barber. The Undertakers move in, pick up the stiffened, splurged bodies and exit. They stop at Bugsy who reverently places a hot towel over Frankie's petrified face. The Violinist has been playing throughout and exits with the Undertakers.

BUGSY   Now, as you can see, something kind of fishy is going on here. To be perfectly honest, I'm beginning to wonder what's going on myself . . . I mean this play's only just started and already the stage is full of stiffs! Oh, by the way, you're probably wondering who I am. My name's Malone, Bugsy Malone.

Questions

1. Find words or phrases to show that:

   a) Roxy Robinson is stupid.

   b) The Hoods are baddies.

   c) Flash Frankie is a good talker.

   d) Bugsy is the hero.

2. This is a play for children. Find words or phrases that show this.

3. What do you think 'splurge' means?

Investigations

Stage directions

The stage directions tell the actors what to do or how to say something. They are printed in italics.

1. Read the stage directions in this extract. Write a list of the actions that take place. Write in chronological order (the order in which they happen).

   > e.g. **Roxy Robinson walks through the audience and gets up onto the stage.**

2. Look at the stage directions again. You will notice that they include directions for sound effects. Next to each sentence in your list, write notes for any sound effects that you need at this point.

3. a) Work in groups. Choose one person's list to work from. Try walking through the actions.

   b) Now keep the actions and add the dialogue. Read from the script as you move. Talk about any difficulties you had. How could you improve your work?

Adverbs

An **adverb** gives us more information about a verb.

Adverbs answer the questions:

- how?
- when?
- where?

How?

adverb   verb

The verb is **run**.

How does he run?

He runs **nervously**.

When?

verb   adverb

The verb is **saw**.

When did they see?

They saw him **yesterday**.

Where?

verb   adverb

The verb is **is happening**.

Where is it happening?

It is happening **here**.

1. Underline the adverbs in the following sentences.

   a) They are going to get Frankie tomorrow.

   b) The Hoods slowly walk towards him.

   c) Roxy Robinson had been truly scrambled.

   d) Flash Frankie is here.

2. Read the passage from the play again and answer these questions.

   a) Many of the adverbs appear in the stage directions. Why do you think this is?

   b) How do the adverbs help the actors?

 Response

Rewrite one of the following episodes as a short story:

- The story of how Roxy the Weasel was trapped and splurged.
- The story of how Flash Frankie was surprised in the barber's shop and splurged.

Remember you will need to describe the actions as well as the dialogue.

 Check!

Remember to use adverbs to show how, when and where things happen.

D2 Applemoon

This is a poem about a mysterious event. It takes place one night in an orchard.

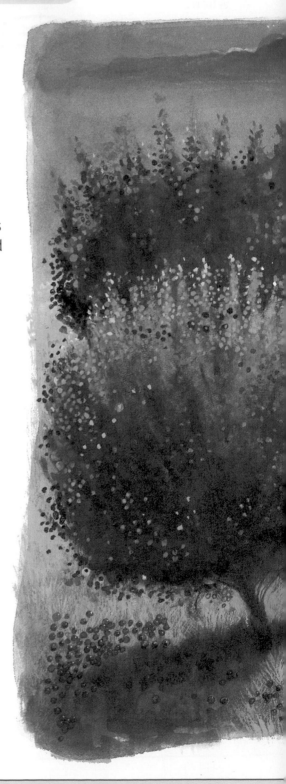

Applemoon

Something woke me: startle-sound
or moonlight. The house dreamt
like an old cat, but I
looked out my window.

And night was day in a midnight
moon-flood. Mazy moon
flaring a halo of quick clouds
running the big black sky.
And I saw a thousand windfall apples
lying luminous as sea-stones beached
below the spiky silver trees.

So, shivering I
mouse-went out
with a basket, barefoot, toes
curling in the cold;
and singing soft
took ripe reluctant apples
under close and curious stars.

Only soon I saw
my shadow was not
the same as I;
it stooped more –
had its own thinness . . .
and our fingers
never met.

I quick-ran back
the house so
sleepy-warm, sure.
But looking out through curtain lace
I saw my shadow linger
moving slow and crooked, plucking
shadow apples
from the shining moony grass.

Rose Flint

Questions

1. Answer these questions.

   a) Who is speaking in the poem?

   b) What words tell you that it is night time?

   c) Why did the speaker go outside?

   d) What made her go back in?

2. What happens in the first three stanzas?

3. What happens in the last two stanzas?

Investigations

Alliteration

Look at the lines:

And night was day in a **m**idnight
moon-flood. **M**azy **m**oon

In these lines, the writer has repeated the sound 'm'. When a writer repeats sounds it is called **alliteration**.

Alliteration can be used to create a certain feeling. For example, lots of 'm' sounds make it feel sleepy and slow – like it is at night.

1. Find three other examples of alliteration in the poem.

2. What does the alliteration make the poem feel like?

Similes

A **simile** is when we compare one thing to another thing using 'as' or 'like'.

e.g. **The house dreamt
<u>like</u> an old cat**

**a thousand windfall apples
lying luminous <u>as</u> sea-stones**

Similes help to make a picture in the reader's mind.

1. Which of the following are similes?

    a) I saw my shadow linger.

    b) My shadow was like a black cloak.

    c) The shadows were as dark as night.

2. Choose a word from column A to compare with a word from column B. Then write a simile for each one. The first one has been done for you.

A	B	
stars	dragon	The stars are like diamonds in the sky.
moon	diamonds	_____
clouds	earthquake	_____
lightning	cheese	_____
thunder	cotton wool	_____

 ## Response

1. Look back at the poem. Which of the following words best describes the poem?

    a) Sinister

    b) Comforting

    c) Mysterious

    d) Puzzling

    e) Dreamy

    f) Unexpected

2. Write a paragraph explaining why you chose this word. Refer to some of the words and phrases in the poem to help you to explain how you made your choice.

D3 Survival

This piece of writing is by Floella Benjamin. Floella came to England from Trinidad in the 1960s. This extract is about what she thought of English weather. Marmie is Floella Benjamin's mother.

Survival

The days and weeks turned into cold winter months and I felt as if my body was going to break. White smoke came out of my mouth as I spoke. I blew on to my fingers to try to warm them but nothing could get rid of the tight, stiff feeling deep inside me. When we first arrived in England I thought it was cold but now I knew what coldness really was. Then there was an orange-gold look about the trees, but now it was freezing and the trees had lost their leaves so they stood naked like skeletons exposing every limb. I wished the cold, grey, misty mornings would go away for I longed to see the warm sun and feel the heat of it on my back, penetrating into my soul.

Word Bank

penetrating: getting into

distorted: changed in some way, out of shape

impenetrable: something you cannot see through or pass through

The wintry weather made me feel depressed. The nights seemed to start so early, even before the end of the afternoons. When we came out of school it was already dark. Once we came out and it seemed as if the world had disappeared under a grey blanket. I couldn't see anything except for fuzzy, distorted lights coming at me out of the distance. People also started to appear from nowhere and disappear again. As I stumbled forward I squinted my eyes in an effort to see more clearly but it made no difference – the thick greyness was impenetrable. There was a hushed, mysterious feel to the atmosphere; even the usual traffic noise was muted as vehicles slowly crawled along the roads, creeping in and out of vision. The cold, sooty air seeped into my lungs and made me cough; it tasted horrible. Later on the radio I heard someone saying that it was one of the foggiest days London had ever seen.

In my short time in England I had experienced all kinds of unpleasant weather: cold winds that felt as if they would tear the skin on my face; freezing rain (not the sort I felt like dancing in); and days upon days without sunlight. I could never be sure what the next day would be like and I began to understand why the English always talked about the weather. There was so much of it.

There was, however, one kind of weather that made me feel happy even though it was cold. I so clearly remember the first time I experienced the thrill of it. On a cold morning, as I huddled under my thick blanket, the smell of the paraffin lamp still lingering in the air, I was awakened by a stillness, an eerie quietness. A strong, clear light shone through the curtains, not the usual murky greyness but a magical light. I sensed something was different about this day as I slowly went to the window. I lifted up the curtains and wiped the condensation off the pane. Then I saw it, a pure white blanket that dazzled me. It was a whiteness I had never seen before and everything was covered in it. I gasped with wonderment. The landscape looked so beautiful, it took my breath away. Surprisingly I didn't feel cold; the beauty had warmed me. I had fallen in love with snow. We spent the rest of the day watching from the windows. Marmie didn't send us to school because it was snowing, but she got told off by the Headmistress who told her that next time we had to come to school in the snow – it would not hurt us, we would survive!

Questions

1. Answer these questions. Use words or phrases from the extract to back up your answers.

   a) How does the writer feel about the weather at the beginning of the extract?

   b) What sort of weather is described in the second paragraph?

   c) Why did vehicles have to crawl slowly along the roads?

   d) Why did Marmie keep her children at home for a day?

2. In the third paragraph, Floella Benjamin writes about the wide variety of weather in England. What does this make you think about the weather in Trinidad? Explain your answer.

3. What word best describes Floella's attitude to the weather in Britain?

hatred	misery	curiosity	mystery	excitement

 ## Investigations

When we compare one thing to another using the words like or as, it is called a simile.

   e.g.   The trees stood naked like skeletons.

When we compare one thing to another by saying it *is* that thing, it is called a metaphor.

   e.g.   The snow was a pure white blanket.

1. In this extract, Floella Benjamin uses similes and metaphors to create a vivid picture of the weather in England.

   a) Why do you think Floella Benjamin says the trees were like skeletons?

   b) Why do you think she says the snow is a blanket?

   c) Find one other simile and one other metaphor in the extract. Write an explanation of each.

2. There are a lot of weather words in English, probably because there is such a variety of weather in England. In your group, make a list of all the weather words you can think of. You could use a dictionary and/or a thesaurus to help you.

   e.g.   drizzle = a very fine rain

3. When you have completed your list of weather words, write a simile for each one.

   e.g.   Drizzle as fine as silk threads.

4. Now turn each simile into a metaphor.

   e.g.   Silk threads of drizzle.

5. Floella Benjamin chooses her words very carefully because she wants her readers to experience the English weather as she does.

   a) Make a list of all the unusual words and phrases she uses.

   e.g.   She uses 'wintry' instead of 'winter'.

   b) Use a dictionary to find the meanings of any unfamiliar words. Choose six words that are new to you. Write sentences containing the new words.

Response

Imagine you are writing to an alien from another planet. There is no weather on your home planet. In four short paragraphs describe:

- Fog
- Hail
- Snow
- A thunderstorm

Check!

Use some of the new words, similes and metaphors in your writing.

D4 The Iceman

'Who was the Iceman?' is a report of a real mystery. On 19 September 1991, the frozen body of a man was found in the Alps. Tests showed that the body was thousands of years old. The man was given the name Ötzi. No one knows for certain who the man was.

Who was the Iceman?

As soon as the Iceman was discovered, people all over the world began wondering who he was. Was he a hunter or shepherd, caught out in a snow storm, or a trader who had lost his way while crossing the Alps? Where had he come from, and where was he going? How had he died, and when? A careful study of Ötzi and his possessions is already beginning to give us the answers.

Some questions can be answered easily. Ötzi was in his late twenties, with swarthy skin, a beard, and dark hair neatly trimmed into the world's oldest haircut. He was quite short – about 1.6 metres – and was tattooed on his back, knee and ankle with lines and crosses. He was well dressed for the cold in a grass cape, leather jacket and trousers, a fur hat and boots stuffed with hay. Ötzi was extremely well equipped for his day. His climbing kit included a copper axe, rope, a leather pouch with a scraper in it, an unstrung bow, and a fur quiver full of unfinished arrows. His backpack contained food supplies including a ripe sloe or plum. This suggests that he probably died in autumn. Whatever he was doing in the Alps, it is clear Ötzi's trip was carefully planned.

Historians believe that Ötzi may have come from one of two different areas of settlement, one in northern Italy between Milan and Venice, the other in southern Switzerland and Austria. Prehistoric villages there were usually built on the edges of lakes. People lived by hunting and simple farming. (Ötzi's worn teeth showed he ate a lot of coarse grain.) Perhaps the Iceman was travelling from one area to the other. At any rate, some time in a long-forgotten prehistoric autumn, he took shelter among the rocks of the Similaun Glacier. Here, overcome by cold, a snow storm or perhaps even ill health, he died.

Although we will probably never know exactly who Ötzi was, the most romantic theory is that he was a shaman or witchdoctor. A number of curious details support this idea. First, the fact that he was carrying a copper axe at a time when most people only had stone means that Ötzi was a person of great importance. Only a chieftain, or a respected priest-magician could be

Word Bank

swarthy:	dark, with a tanned skin
quiver:	something to carry arrows in
rituals:	formal ceremonies
hallucinogens:	drugs that make people see things that are not really there

expected to have what was, in 3300 BC, such new technology. Second, mountains are traditionally sacred. The Iceman's body was found quite close to a place still regarded in local folklore as a holy site. The fact that Ötzi's weapons were virtually useless (the arrows, for example, had no tips) suggests that they were for rituals, rather than hunting or fighting. And finally, the mushrooms in his pouch – which experts initially thought were tinder for fires – were powerful hallucinogens, eaten to induce visions of gods, spirits, or perhaps even the future.

Questions

1. Look carefully at the description of Ötzi in the second paragraph. Then look at the lists below. Draw lines to match the correct adjective to the noun it describes. The first one has been done for you.

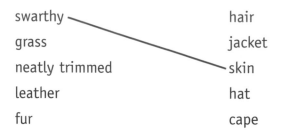

swarthy	hair
grass	jacket
neatly trimmed	skin
leather	hat
fur	cape

2. Answer the questions below:

   a) How do we know that Ötzi's trip was carefully planned?

   b) What sort of food did Ötzi eat?

   c) Where did Ötzi find shelter from the weather?

   d) What is another word for 'shaman'?

3. Look at the title of the passage.

   a) Why has the writer used a question as a title?

   b) Do you think this is a good title? Explain your answer.

Investigations

1. How many paragraphs are there in this passage?

2. Look at the first paragraph. There are three questions asked in this paragraph. What are they?

3. Look at the first question you found.

   a) Is there an answer to this question?

   b) Where is it discussed?

4. Look at the second question you found.

   a) Is there an answer to this question?

   b) Where is it discussed?

5. Look at the third question you found.

   a) Is there an answer to this question?

   b) Where is it discussed?

6. Write a topic sentence for each paragraph.

7. Write a plan for this text. Look at the plan for your story in the Response section below to help you.

 Response

Write a story describing what happened to the Iceman. Use this plan to help you.

Plan

Paragraph 1 – The Iceman begins his journey.

- Where was he going?
- Why?
- What did he take with him?

Paragraph 2 – The Iceman meets someone.

- Who was this person?
- What did he/she look like?
- What did he/she say?

Paragraph 3 – Bad weather sets in.

- Where is the Iceman?
- What does he think?
- What does he do?

Paragraph 4 – The Iceman dies.

- What were his last thoughts?

 Check!

Remember to write in paragraphs and to link each paragraph together.

D5 Lost for Words

This piece of writing is about a family from Bangladesh who have come to live in London. Aysha and her mother, Ama, are living in a run-down house in London. One night, they are woken by the sound of a fire.

Word Bank

sari: a length of cloth wrapped around the body

dupatta: a long scarf worn over the head

Aysha put her arm around her mother's shoulder, pulled her coat more tightly round her thin sari and drew the dupatta up over Ama's hair. It was all she could do. She didn't know what she could say.

They stood together at the window, staring out at the bright, flickering light as if they were still asleep and dreaming. The strange, wind-like noise broke and fell like waves across the back yards outside. Aysha knew the yards, full of dustbins and rusting old barbecues and rubbish and cats. She knew they were there even though she couldn't see them, and that was all part of the dream. Aysha felt warm and relaxed as they gazed at the flickering light. A wind like that, a warm wind that bathed them in heat and light in this cold, grey city could only be part of a dream.

There was a crash downstairs, down where the kitchen and the toilet near the back door jutted so far out into the back yard that they almost touched the back wall of the houses in the next street down. Aysha left her mother standing near the bedroom window. Downstairs, the window in the toilet had been blown in and broken glass lay all over the floor. And suddenly the heat was intense. The warm wind was a roaring dragon, spitting out flames. Aysha reached for the metal handle of the back door and screamed as the heat of it blistered her hand.

'Aysha? Who's there?'

Her mother came slowly down the stairs, staring into the darkness.

'Aysha? Are you still there?'

Aysha stopped herself crying. She wiped her eyes on the sleeve of her anorak and rushed along the passage to keep her mother away from the back of the house. Then she put her left hand through her mother's arm and pulled Ama towards the front door, speaking calmly, as if to a small child she wanted to stay calm.

'We have to go out, Ama. We can't stay here. There's a fire.'

And Ama let herself be led outside.

continued on page 92

There was no fire in their house. There was no fire the whole length of the street. But the street was full of people standing at their front gates, talking to neighbours they'd never spoken to in years.

'You wouldn't catch me out the back there. It's enough to singe your eyebrows off,' a man in a black beret was shouting to a woman across the road. 'The windows along our backs are all blown in. My wife was standing there looking out and I told her not to be such an old fool. That's why we come out here. And two minutes later, the back bedroom window . . . Right where she was standing. The back bedroom window was all blown in.' Aysha couldn't see the man's wife. And she could only just see his silhouette. He had glasses on, and a beard jutted out below his black hat.

A woman from the house next door leaned over the hedge.

'Are you all right, love? It's right behind you. Any damage?'

Aysha smiled. 'Yes. All right.'

The woman's hands were shaking. She rolled a thin cigarette, lit it and then took a deep breath of the smoke, as if the smoke in the air wasn't enough. 'My boyfriend's gone round to have a look.'

Then a man ran up the street. He had a pony tail and swung himself in at the gate where the woman still dragged at her cigarette. He pulled it out of her mouth and breathed in and out with the thin cigarette between his own lips, still out of breath from running round the block to the street just behind theirs.

He spat the cigarette out on to the floor. 'It's that house where the Tamils were living. Petrol bomb through the letter box. There were seven men in there, all asleep. They won't find anyone alive.' He squashed the cigarette with his foot and stamped on it over and over again. 'They didn't stand a chance.'

Questions

1. Look at the following sentences from the passage. Write down what each one tells you about Aysha.

    a) Aysha put her arm around her mother's shoulder, pulled her coat more tightly round her thin sari and drew the dupatta up over Ama's hair.

    b) Aysha felt warm and relaxed as they gazed at the flickering light.

    c) Aysha stopped herself crying.

    d) ...speaking calmly, as if to a small child she wanted to stay calm.

2. What do you think happened to the Tamils?

3. How do you think the man with the pony tail feels about the fire? Find words from the passage to explain your answer.

Investigations

In Unit C2 *What I Watch*, we saw that sometimes a writer will join simple sentences together to make longer sentences. These are called **multiple sentences**.

1. Read the following sentences from the passage. Which sentences are simple sentences and which are multiple sentences?

    a) Then a man ran up the street.

    b) He squashed the cigarette with his foot and stamped on it over and over again.

    c) We can't stay here.

    d) Ama let herself be led outside.

    e) He had glasses on, and a beard jutted out below his black hat.

> ## Help
>
> A clause is a group of words with only one verb or verb phrase.
>
> e.g.   Then a man <u>ran</u> up the street.
>
> A simple sentence is a sentence with only one clause.
>
> e.g.   Suddenly the heat <u>was</u> intense.
>
> A multiple sentence contains more than one clause.
>
> e.g.   She <u>wiped</u> her eyes on the sleeve of her anorak and <u>rushed</u> along the passage.

Multiple sentences can be **compound sentences** or **complex sentences**.

Compound sentences are often made up by connecting clauses with these connectives:

and	or	but

2. Connect the following clauses to make compound sentences using *and*, *but* or *or*. You may have to leave out some words in your new sentences. The first one has been done for you.

    a) Aysha put her arm around her mother. She pulled her coat round her sari.

    Aysha put her arm around her mother and pulled her coat round her sari.

    b) The window had been blown in. Broken glass lay on the floor.

    c) They were in danger. Aysha wasn't scared.

    d) They could go out of the front. They could go out of the back.

We make **complex sentences** by joining two different types of clause: a main clause and a subordinate clause.

A **main clause** is a clause that makes sense on its own.

> e.g.   Aysha knew the yards.

A **subordinate clause** does not make sense on its own.

> e.g.   which were full of dustbins.

We often use commas to separate the main clause from the subordinate clause.

> e.g.   Aysha knew the yards, which were full of dustbins.

3. Read the following complex sentences. Underline the main clause in each sentence. The first one has been done for you.

   a) <u>They stood together at the window</u>, while they stared out at the bright light.

   b) Aysha felt warm and relaxed as they gazed at the flickering light.

   c) She wiped her eyes before she rushed along the passage.

   d) Although there was no fire in the street, a lot of people were outside.

4. Join a main clause to a subordinate clause to make a complex sentence.

Main clause	Subordinate clause
a) They had to go outside	i) who was her mother.
b) Aysha looked after Ama	ii) after he ran down the road.
c) The man said the Tamils' house was on fire	iii) as he was angry.
d) He stamped his foot	iv) because there was a fire.

5. In this passage the writer uses a mixture of simple, compound and complex sentences. Read the last paragraph and answer the following questions:

   a) How many simple sentences are there?

   b) How many compound sentences are there?

   c) How many complex sentences are there?

   d) Why do you think the writer chose to use so many simple sentences in this paragraph?

Response

Imagine you are the man with the pony tail. Write your diary entry for the night of the fire, telling what happened, what you saw and how you felt.

Check!

Remember to use a mixture of simple, compound and complex sentences to make your writing more interesting.

Test Yourself!

In this section, you have learnt about:
- adverbs
- alliteration
- similes
- metaphors
- paragraphs
- multiple sentences.

Answer the following questions to check you have understood what you have learnt.

1. Which of the following are similes and which are metaphors?

   a) The snow was a pure white blanket.

   b) The daffodils waved like flags.

   c) The trees looked like skeletons

   d) The clouds were like cotton wool.

2. Which of the following are simple sentences and which are multiple sentences?

   a) Someone had put a petrol bomb through the letter box.

   b) Everyone in the street came out to watch, although the fire was a long way away.

   c) A man came running, while he shouted out, 'Fire!'

   d) Aysha helped her mother out of the house.

   e) She was not afraid, but her mother was.

3. Underline the main clause in the following complex sentences.

   a) When she heard the noise, Aysha got up.

   b) She led her mother to the street, where there were lots of people.

   c) The man told them the Tamils' house had caught fire after it was attacked.

   d) Aysha's mother was scared because she didn't know what was happening.

Section E
Our World

The pieces of writing in this section are all about the world we live in. Some are about everyday events and some are about mysterious events.

In this section, you will learn about:

- using adjectives
- personal pronouns
- Standard English and dialect
- the subject and object of a sentence
- subject-verb agreement
- building up tension.

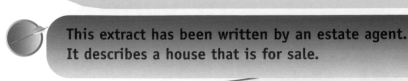

This extract has been written by an estate agent. It describes a house that is for sale.

The Cottage

PURCHASE PRICE £89,000

DESCRIPTION

An attractive colour-washed white cottage under a pitched tiled roof and with dormer windows to the first floor. Wooden framed casement and sash-type windows.

The cottage is located close to the beach and sea and is very convenient for the High Street and shops and would form an ideal cottage for weekend and holiday use.

Aldeburgh is a popular holiday town. It is well known for its annual Festival of Music and the Arts which normally takes place in June. The Snape Maltings Hall Concert Hall Complex is located a short motoring distance inland with sailing on the river at Slaughden. There are also two golf courses within a short motoring distance of the property, one in Aldeburgh, the other at Thorpeness.

The nearest railway station is at Saxmundham, some seven miles distant, with trains to London Liverpool Street via Ipswich (also trains to Lowestoft). There is a bus service from Aldeburgh to the county town of Ipswich, which is some 25 miles distant.

The accommodation is on two floors and is approached via a porch with flat felted roof and with a wooden stable-type front door. Step down to the

LIVING ROOM
which measures about 14'6" x 14' and into the small dining area. Large attractive brick fireplace with mantleshelf over. Coal effect gas fire.

Exposed beams to the ceiling and walls. Oil filled electrically heated radiator with Dimplex electric storage heater. Staircase to the first floor. Three wrought iron wall lights. Two strip lights to the small dining area. To one side of the fireplace there is an alcove with cupboard which houses the electrical switchgear and meter. White painted built–in chest with eight short drawers.

From the rear of the Living Room two steps up to a white painted door to the rear Hall with rear stable-type external door. Sliding door through to the

KITCHEN

with worktop, circular sink unit, hot and cold mixer tap, tiled splashback, short drawers with shelved cupboards under. Shelving with curtain front and gas meter. Worktop. Inset to the worktop is a Baby Belling two burner electric cooker. Refrigerator. Wall mounted grill marked Cannon. Fluorescent ceiling light. Fan assisted Dimplex electric heater. One single and one double wall cupboard.

From the rear Hall a low narrow door leads through to the

BATHROOM

with electric towel heater. Panelled bath, hot and cold taps, decorated tiled splashback. Low level w.c. suite. Pedestal basin, hot and cold taps, decorated tiled splashback. Wall mounted Dimplex fan assisted electric wall heater. Strip light over the basin.

From the rear of the Living Room cottage-type staircase with shelf and double glazed velux-type roof light. White painted stable-type door and step up to the

BEDROOM

which measures about 11'9" x 12'6" with storage alcove, wardrobe cupboard, electrically heated oil filled radiator. Dormer window. Slatted shelving housing the combination hot and cold water cylinder with electric immersion heater. The bedroom has a sloping ceiling to the front and rear.

OUTSIDE

to the front brick stub wall on King Street with concreted area. Small rear concreted courtyard with corrugated plastic roof. Storage shed with shelving, electric light, water stop tap and drainage connection. Gate and right of way over path to King Street.

SERVICES

Mains electricity, water and drainage.

Questions

1. Choose the correct answer to the following questions:

    a) Where is the cottage located?

        i)   in the countryside

        ii) near the beach and sea

        iii) next to the golf course.

    b) What is the town of Aldeburgh well known for?

        i)   holidays

        ii) Festival of Music and Arts

        iii) The Snape Maltings Hall Concert Hall Complex.

    c) How do you get to London by train from Aldeburgh?

        i)   via Ipswich

        ii) via Lowestoft

        iii) via Thorpeness.

2. Write down the words or phrases that tell you that:

    a) the living room is below street level

    b) the bathroom is on the ground floor

    c) there is no garden.

3. Would you like to live in this cottage? Why or why not?

Investigations

The writer of this extract is trying to sell the cottage. He is trying to make it seem as attractive as possible. He uses lots of adjectives to make the place seem appealing.

Using adjectives

1. Read the paragraph which describes the living room. Fill in the table on page 101 to show which adjectives describe each of the nouns. Some nouns have more than one adjective.

Help

An adjective describes a noun (see page 35).

e.g.   The <u>pretty</u> cottage is in the <u>busy</u> town.

Noun	Adjective
fireplace	_____
gas fire	_____
beams	_____
radiator	_____
wall lights	_____
chest	_____
drawers	_____

2. Now look at the paragraph describing the bathroom. Make your own table showing the nouns, and the adjectives that describe each noun.

Noun	Adjective
_____	_____
_____	_____
_____	_____

Response

Imagine the house or flat where you live is being sold. Create an estate agent's leaflet to sell your home. Follow this plan to help you.

Plan

1. Describe the area around your house/flat. What is the place famous for? Are there any places of interest, public transport, etc?

2. Describe each room in turn.

3. Describe any land you have around your home.

Check!

Remember to use adjectives that make your home seem attractive.

E2 Zlata's Diary

This extract is taken from the diary of Zlata Filipovic. She was a young girl who lived through the war in Sarajevo.

Saturday, 2 May 1992

Dear Mimmy,

Today was truly, absolutely the worst day ever in Sarajevo. The shooting started around noon. Mummy and I moved into the hall. Daddy was in his office, under our flat, at the time. We told him on the interphone to run quickly to the downstairs lobby where we'd meet him. We brought Cicko [Zlata's canary] with us. The gunfire was getting worse, and we couldn't get over the wall to the Bobars, so we ran down to our own cellar.

The cellar is ugly, dark, smelly. Mummy, who's terrified of mice, had two fears to cope with. The three of us were in the same corner as the other day. We listened to the pounding shells, the shooting, the thundering noise overhead. We even heard planes. At one moment I realised that this awful cellar was the only place that could save our lives. Suddenly, it started to look almost warm and nice. It was the only way we could defend ourselves against all this terrible shooting. We heard glass shattering in our street. Horrible. I put my fingers in my ears to block out the terrible sounds. I was worried about Cicko. We had left him behind in the lobby. Would he catch cold there? Would something hit him? I was terribly hungry and thirsty. We had left our half-cooked lunch in the kitchen.

When the shooting died down a bit, Daddy ran over to our flat and brought us back some sandwiches. He said he could smell something burning and that the phones weren't working. He brought our TV set down to the cellar. That's when we learned that the main post office (near us) was on fire and that they had kidnapped our President. At around 20.00 we went back up to our flat. Almost every window in our street was broken. Ours were all right, thank God. I saw the post office in flames. A terrible sight. The fire-fighters battled with the raging fire. Daddy took a few photos of the post office being devoured by the flames. He said they wouldn't come out because I had been fiddling with something on the camera. I was sorry. The whole flat smelled of the burning fire. God, and I used to pass by there every day. It had just been done up. It was huge and beautiful, and now it was being swallowed up by the flames. It was disappearing. That's what this neighbourhood of mine looks like, dear Mimmy. I wonder what it's like in other parts of town? I heard on the radio that it was awful around the Eternal Flame. The place is knee-deep in glass. We're worried about Grandma and Grandad. They live there. Tomorrow, if we can go out, we'll see how they are. A terrible day. This has been the worst, most awful day in my eleven-year-old life. I hope it will be the only one.

Mummy and Daddy are very edgy. I have to go to bed.

Ciao!

Tuesday, 18 August 1992

Dear Mimmy,

Mummy is carrying home the water. It's hard on her, but she has to do it. The water hasn't come back on. Nor has the electricity.

I didn't tell you, Mimmy, but I've forgotten what it's like to have water pouring out of a tap, what it's like to have a shower. We use a jug now. The jug has replaced the shower. We wash dishes and clothes like in the Middle Ages. This war is taking us back to olden times. And we take it, we suffer it, but we don't know for how long.

Zlata

Wednesday, 6 January 1993

Dear Mimmy,

It's freezing. Winter has definitely come to town. I used to love and enjoy it so much, but now it's a very disagreeable guest in Sarajevo.

Our flowers have frozen. They were in the rooms we didn't heat. We live in the kitchen now. That's the only room we heat and we manage to get the temperature up to 17°C. Cicko is with us. I'm afraid he might get sick, because birds are sensitive to winter.

We moved the mattresses into the kitchen and now we sleep here. (Don't make me tell you how many sweaters and pullovers we wear over our pyjamas.) The kitchen is now our kitchen and our sitting room and our bedroom and even our bathroom. We have an unusual way of bathing. We spread out the sheets of plastic and then – the basin becomes our bathtub, the jug our shower, and so on.

Daddy's got frostbite on his fingers from cutting the wood in the cold cellar. They look awful. His fingers are swollen and now they're putting some cream on them, but they itch badly. Poor Daddy.

Tomorrow I'm probably going to Grandma's and Grandad's. They have gas heating.

Zlata

Questions

1. How can you tell from the layout of the text that you are reading a diary?

2. Explain in your own words how Zlata and her family keep clean.

3. Complete the following table. In column A are some of the things that Zlata writes about. In column B, write down how Zlata felt about each thing. In column C write down words from the passage that tell you how Zlata felt. The first one has been done for you.

Column A	Column B	Column C
Things Zlata writes about	**How Zlata felt**	**How you know**
The cellar when they first went into it	Zlata hated the cellar	ugly, dark, smelly
The cellar after the shells started	_____	_____
Cicko	_____	_____
The post office in flames	_____	_____
Grandma and Grandad	_____	_____
Daddy's frostbite	_____	_____

Investigations

In a diary, the writer is often writing about their own feelings. Diary writers often use a lot of **personal pronouns** in their writing because they know the people involved and want to keep the writing very personal.

A **personal pronoun** is a word that can be used instead of a noun.

These are some personal pronouns:

I	you	he	she	it	we	they
me	you	him	her	it	us	them

1. Read the following sentences. Replace the nouns with suitable pronouns from the list at the bottom of page 104.

   a) Mummy is carrying home the water. It's hard on Mummy, but Mummy has to do it.

   b) Zlata's canary was left upstairs so Zlata was worried about the canary.

   c) Zlata went to see Grandma and Grandad because Zlata was worried about Grandma and Grandad.

   d) Daddy's finger got frostbite so Daddy's fingers were swollen.

2. Now read the diary entry for Tuesday 18 August. How many personal pronouns can you find?

Response

Imagine that you are Zlata's father and that you have also kept a diary. Write your diary entry for 2 May 1992 describing what has happened. Follow the points below to help you.

   a) Begin by talking in groups about what Zlata's father would have:

   • seen

   • heard

   • thought.

   e.g. **Zlata's father was working in his office when the shooting started. He answered the interphone and spoke to either Zlata or her mother.**

   b) When you have come up with a list of the things that happened, think about how Zlata's father would have felt.

   e.g. **How did he feel when he found out Zlata had broken the camera?**

   c) Now write Zlata's father's diary. Write in the first person (use 'I') and include details of how he was feeling.

Check!

Remember to use personal pronouns as appropriate.

Read the following poem aloud.

Baby-K Rap Rhyme

My name is Baby-K
An dis is my rhyme
Sit back folks
While I rap my mind;

Ah rocking with my homegirl,
My Mommy
Ah rocking with my homeboy,
My Daddy
My big sister, Les, an
My Granny,
Hey dere people – my posse
I'm the business
The ruler of the nursery

poop po-doop
poop-poop po-doop
poop po-doop
poop-poop po-doop

Well, ah soaking up de rhythm
Ah drinking up my tea
Ah bouncing an ah rocking
On my Mommy knee
So happy man so happy

poop po-doop
poop-poop po-doop
poop po-doop
poop-poop po-doop

Wish my rhyme wasn't hard
Wish my rhyme wasn't rough
But sometimes, people
You got to be tough

Cause dey pumping up de
chickens
Dey stumping down de trees
Dey messing up de ozones
Dey messing up de seas
Baby-K say, stop dis –
please, please, please

Cause dey hotting up de globe,
man
Dey hitting down de seals
Dey killing off de ellies
for dere ivories
Baby-K say, stop dis –
please, please, please

poop po-doop
poop-poop po-doop
poop po-doop
poop-poop po-doop

poop po-doop
poop-poop po-doop
poop po-doop
poop-poop po-doop

Now am splashing in de bath
With my rubber duck
Who don't like dis rhyme
Kiss my baby-foot
Babies everywhere
Join a Babyhood

Dis is my Baby-K rap
But it's kinda plea
What kinda world
Dey going to leave fuh me?
What kinda world
Dey going to leave fuh me?

Poop po-doop.

Grace

Questions

1. Find two examples from the poem of each of the following:

    a) an ordinary baby activity

    b) an issue that concerns the environment.

2. Look at the stanzas in italics. They are like the chorus to a song. Why do you think Grace Nichols (the poet) has included these stanzas?

3. Read the final four lines.

    a) Why do you think Grace Nichols repeats the question?

    b) What does Grace Nichols think the answer to the question is?

Investigations

Grace Nichols uses some words and phrases that people might say instead of using **Standard English**. This is called speaking in **dialect**.

> e.g.   'ellies'
>
>   instead of
>
>   'elephants'

She has also written some words as they sound rather than using the correct spelling.

1. Look at these words from the poem. What is the correct spelling for each word?

    a) an
    b) dis
    c) dere
    d) ah
    e) de

2. Why do you think Grace Nichols has written like this?

Grace Nichols has also missed out certain words to make the lines sound like speech.

e.g.   **Cause dey hotting up de globe, man**

instead of

Cause dey <u>are</u> hotting up de globe, man

3. Find three other examples of sentences that are not in Standard English.

4. Now choose one stanza and rewrite it in Standard English using conventional spelling and sentences. The first stanza has been done for you as an example.

    My name is Baby-K

    And this is my song

    Sit back everyone

    While I use rap to tell you what I am thinking;

5. Read aloud the version you have written and the original version. Which do you prefer? Why?

 ## Response

A rap is written to be read aloud. Prepare a group performance of this poem.

1. First think about how you will divide up the lines.

    a) Which lines should be read by more than one person?

    b) Which lines should be read by everyone?

    c) Which lines should be read by one person?

2. Decide whether you need any background sound, such as clapping or beating a drum to help you to keep the rhythm.

3. How will you keep your audience interested throughout the performance of the poem?

    a) Which parts of the poem are the most important and need the most emphasis?

    b) How can you give them emphasis?

    c) Can you speed up or slow down?

    d) Can you get louder or softer?

Above all, think about what the poem means to you and aim to show your feelings about the poem in the performance.

E4 The Secret Diary of Adrian Mole Aged 13 $\frac{3}{4}$

Unlike the extract from Zlata's Diary, *The Secret Diary of Adrian Mole Aged 13 $\frac{3}{4}$* is completely made up. It is about a teenage boy.

The Secret Diary of Adrian Mole Aged 13 $\frac{3}{4}$ by Sue Townsend

Thursday January 1st
BANK HOLIDAY IN ENGLAND, IRELAND, SCOTLAND AND WALES

These are my New Year's resolutions:

1. I will help the blind across the road.
2. I will hang my trousers up.
3. I will put the sleeves back on my records.
4. I will not start smoking.
5. I will stop squeezing my spots.
6. I will be kind to the dog.
7. I will help the poor and ignorant.
8. After hearing the disgusting noises from downstairs last night, I have also vowed never to drink alcohol.

My father got the dog drunk on cherry brandy at the party last night. If the RSPCA hear about it he could get done. Eight days have gone by since Christmas Day but my mother still hasn't worn the green lurex apron I bought her for Christmas! She will get bathcubes next year.

Just my luck, I've got a spot on my chin for the first day of the New Year!

Friday January 2nd
BANK HOLIDAY IN SCOTLAND, FULL MOON

I felt rotten today. It's my mother's fault for singing 'My Way' at two o'clock in the morning at the top of the stairs. Just my luck to have a mother like her. There is a chance my parents could be alcoholics. Next year I could be in a children's home.

Word Bank

lurex:	a type of material
rigging:	the ropes on a ship that hold the sails up
scurvy:	a disease caused by not enough vitamin C

The dog got its own back on my father. It jumped up and knocked down his model ship, then ran into the garden with the rigging tangled in its feet. My father kept saying, 'Three months' work down the drain', over and over again.

The spot on my chin is getting bigger. It's my mother's fault for not knowing about vitamins.

Saturday January 3rd

I shall go mad through lack of sleep! My father has banned the dog from the house so it barked outside my window all night. Just my luck! My father shouted a swear-word at it. If he's not careful he will get done by the police for obscene language.

I think the spot is a boil. Just my luck to have it where everybody can see it. I pointed out to my mother that I hadn't had any vitamin C today. She said, 'Go and buy an orange, then'. This is typical.

She still hasn't worn the lurex apron.

I will be glad to get back to school.

Sunday January 4th
SECOND AFTER CHRISTMAS

My father has got the flu. I'm not surprised with the diet we get. My mother went out in the rain to get him a vitamin C drink, but as I told her, 'It's too late now'. It's a miracle we don't get scurvy. My mother says she can't see anything on my chin, but this is guilt because of the diet.

The dog has run off because my mother didn't close the gate. I have broken the arm on the stereo. Nobody knows yet, and with a bit of luck my father will be ill for a long time. He is the only one who uses it apart from me. No sign of the apron.

Word Bank

meter-reader: traffic warden

Monday January 5th

The dog hasn't come back yet. It is peaceful without it. My mother rang the police and gave a description of the dog. She made it sound worse than it actually is: straggly hair over its eyes and all that. I really think the police have got better things to do than look for dogs, such as catching murderers. I told my mother this but she still rang them. Serve her right if she was murdered because of the dog.

My father is still lazing about in bed. He is supposed to be ill, but I noticed he is still smoking!

Nigel came round today. He has got a tan from his Christmas holiday. I think Nigel will be ill soon from the shock of the cold in England. I think Nigel's parents were wrong to take him abroad.

He hasn't got a single spot yet.

Tuesday January 6th
Epiphany, New Moon

The dog is in trouble!

It knocked a meter-reader off his bike and messed all the cards up. So now we will all end up in court I expect. A policeman said we must keep the dog under control and asked how long it had been lame. My mother said it wasn't lame, and examined it. There was a tiny model pirate trapped in his left front paw.

The dog was pleased when my mother took the pirate out and it jumped up the policeman's tunic with its muddy paws. My mother fetched a cloth from the kitchen but it had strawberry jam on it where I had wiped the knife, so the tunic was worse than ever. The policeman went then. I'm sure he swore. I could report him for that.

I will look up 'Epiphany' in my new dictionary.

Questions

1. Put Adrian's New Year's resolutions into two groups. Group 1 includes those about his personal habits. Group 2 includes those about helping others.

Group 1: Personal habits	Group 2: Helping others
_____	_____
_____	_____
_____	_____
_____	_____

2. Complete the following sentences.

   a) Adrian thinks his mother is...

   b) Adrian thinks his father is...

3. Which of these words best describes Adrian Mole? Use words and phrases from the extract to explain your choice.

worried	impatient	loving	anxious	kind	irritated

 # Investigations

Subject

A sentence must have a verb.

The person or thing that does the verb is called the **subject** of the sentence.

e.g.

Subject   Verb

The verb is **ran**.

Who ran?

The dog ran.

So **the dog** is the subject.

Underline the verbs in these sentences. Then ask who or what is doing each verb. That person or thing is the subject. Circle the subject in each sentence.

a) I will help the blind.

b) My father has got the flu.

c) My mother has not worn her apron.

d) The dog drank cherry brandy.

Object

The object of the sentence is the person or thing the verb is done to.

e.g. (I will help)(the blind.)

subject   verb   object

The verb is **will help**.

Who will help?

I will, so **I** is the subject.

Who will I help?

The blind, so **the blind** is the object.

Look at the sentences in the question above. What is the object in each sentence?

Subject-verb agreement

1. Now read the following sentences. What is the verb in each sentence and what is the subject?

a) I run into the garden.   e) It runs into the garden.

b) You run into the garden.   f) We run into the garden.

c) He runs into the garden.   g) You run into the garden.

d) She runs into the garden.   h) They run into the garden.

2. What do you notice about the verb when the subject changes? The verb changes:

● depending on the **person** doing the verb.

e.g.   I run (1st person)
        he runs (3rd person)

● depending on the **number** of people doing the verb

e.g.   he runs (singular: one person)
        they run (plural: more than one person).

This is called subject-verb agreement.

3. The following sentences all have mistakes in the subject-verb agreement. Read the sentences and underline the mistakes.

    a) It are my mother's fault.

    b) She sing 'My Way' every morning.

    c) My parents am drinking too much.

    d) I needs more attention.

    e) My diet are suffering.

4. Now write out the correct version of the sentences in question 2.

5. Fill in the blanks in the following passage with the correct form of the verb in brackets.

    Adrian (be) _____ a teenage boy.

    He (live) _____ with his parents.

    They (have) _____ a dog.

    His father (hate) _____ the dog.

    You (learn) _____ all about Adrian through his diary.

    It (be) _____ very funny.

 Response

Choose one of the characters from the extract:

- Adrian's mother
- Adrian's father
- The meter-reader

Write a diary entry for your character. Start at the beginning of the New Year, with a list of New Year's resolutions. Write about what happened that day and how you plan to start the New Year.

 Check!

When you have finished, check that all the verbs in your sentences agree with the subject of that sentence.

E5 Skellig

Skellig is a wonderful story about a strange creature that lives in an old garage. Skellig is written by David Almond (see Section A, Unit 1). Michael and his family have moved into an old house. Michael's baby sister is very ill. One day, while the doctor is visiting, Michael explores the old garage.

Skellig

I finished the Coke, waited a minute, then I went down to the garage again. I didn't have time to dare myself or to stand there listening to the scratching. I switched the torch on, took a deep breath, and tiptoed straight inside.

Something little and black scuttled across the floor. The door creaked and cracked for a moment before it was still. Dust poured through the torch beam. Something scratched and scratched in a corner. I tiptoed further in and felt spider webs breaking on my brow. Everything was packed in tight – ancient furniture, kitchen units, rolled-up carpets, pipes and crates and planks. I kept ducking down under the hose-pipes and ropes and kitbags that hung from the roof. More cobwebs snapped on my clothes and skin. The floor was broken and crumbly. I opened a cupboard an inch, shone the torch in and saw a million woodlice scattering away. I peered down into a great stone jar and saw the bones of some little animal that had died in there. Dead bluebottles were everywhere. There were ancient newspapers and magazines. I shone the torch on to one and saw that it came from nearly fifty years ago. I moved so carefully. I was scared every moment that the whole thing was going to collapse. There was dust clogging my throat and nose. I knew they'd be yelling for me soon and I knew I'd better get out. I leaned across a heap of tea chests and shone the torch into the space behind and that's when I saw him.

I thought he was dead. He was sitting with his legs stretched out, and his head tipped back against the wall. He was covered in dust and webs like everything else and his face was thin and pale. Dead bluebottles were scattered on his hair and shoulders. I shone the torch on his white face and his black suit.

'What do you want?' he said.

He opened his eyes and looked up at me.

His voice squeaked like he hadn't used it in years.

'What do you want?'

My heart thudded and thundered.

'I said, what do you want?'

Then I heard them yelling for me from the house.

'Michael! Michael! Michael!'

I shuffled out again. I backed out through the door.

It was Dad. He came down the path to me.

'Didn't we tell you—' he started.

'Yes,' I said. 'Yes. Yes.'

I started to brush the dust off myself. A spider dropped away from my chin on a long string.

He put his arm around me.

'It's for your own good,' he said.

He picked a dead bluebottle out of my hair.

He thumped the side of the garage and the whole thing shuddered.

'See?' he said. 'Imagine what might happen.'

I grabbed his arm to stop him thumping it again.

'Don't,' I said. 'It's all right. I understand.'

He squeezed my shoulder and said everything would be better soon.

He laughed.

'Get all that dust off before your mother sees, eh?'

Questions

1. Answer these questions.

   a) Why did Michael think the creature was dead?

   b) Why did the creature's voice squeak?

   c) Why do you think Michael 'backed out' through the door?

   d) Why does Michael try to stop his Dad thumping the garage?

2. a) How did Michael feel when the creature spoke?

   b) What words tell you this?

3. How would you feel if you saw this creature in your garage? Write a paragraph describing how you would feel.

Investigations

Building up tension

Writers often build up tension to keep their readers' interest or to surprise or shock their reader.

In this passage, David Almond builds up the tension in this passage until Michael finds the creature. We know something is going to happen and we keep reading to find out what. How does David Almond do this? Read the list of ways he builds up tension below.

- He moves around the garage describing all the details before he focuses on one place

- He uses words and phrases to show that Michael is afraid

- He uses long sentences when describing the scene

- He uses short sentences to describe Michael's feelings.

1. Find one example from the passage for each of the ways of building up tension listed above.

2. Look at these verbs from the passage.

> creaked   scratched   cracked   **thudded**   **thundered**

These verbs all describe sounds. How do these sounds make you feel?

3 Find three other verbs in the passage and write down how they make you feel.

Help

A verb tells us what someone or something is doing, feeling or thinking.

e.g. He <u>thumped</u> the side of the garage.

I <u>shuffled</u> out again.

Response

Write your own story in which a character finds something unusual. Remember to hold your readers' attention by building up the tension. First think about what the creature is like.

> e.g. **a man who looks dead**
>
> **an animal with two heads**
>
> **a tiny person**

Then decide where it will be found.

> e.g. **in a garage**
>
> **in a barn**
>
> **in the bike sheds**

Use the following notes to help you.

- begin slowly with lots of detail about the place
- when you find the creature describe it in three short words
- show how your character feels about the creature in short sentences.

Test Yourself!

Answer the following questions to check you have understood what you have learnt.

1. Fill in the blanks in these sentences with personal pronouns from the box below.

    a) As it was cold, _____ moved their mattresses into the kitchen.

    b) Zlata's mother carried the water. _____ had to do it every day.

    c) Zlata' father's got frostbite. _____ was in a lot of pain.

    d) The canary was left upstairs, so Zlata was worried about _____ .

they	it	he	she

2. What is the subject and what is the object in these sentences:

    a) Adrian Mole writes a diary.

    b) His father drinks cherry brandy.

    c) The dog knocked over the model ship.

    d) The dog attacked the meter-reader.

3. The verb does not agree with the subject in these sentences. Write each sentence out correctly.

    a) I hates New Year's resolutions.

    b) My father always have the same ones.

    c) He never keep them.

    d) This year I is not making any.

Section F
The Sea

The extracts in this section are all about the sea or sea voyages.

In this section, you will learn about:

- layout
- characterisation
- using paragraphs
- allegories
- metaphors
- narrator's point of view.

This piece of writing is a factual account of real pirates. Unlike many pirates in stories, these people were unpleasant and dangerous.

Atlantic Storms

The north-western coasts of Europe are rugged, pounded by Atlantic breakers. There are many small inlets, remote islands and secret caves – ideal territory for smugglers and pirates. In the Middle Ages, piracy was common in Scotland, Ireland, Wales, the Isle of Man, the Scilly Isles and Brittany.

To the east, the English Channel, North Sea and Baltic were unsafe for shipping. These were lawless times. For many people, piracy seemed a fair way to attack enemies and rivals, or to gain wealth. Many powerful and respectable families organised pirate crews.

Queen of Clew Bay

Gráinne Ni Mháille, or Gráinne Mhaol, was known to the English as Grace O'Malley. This Irish noblewoman, born in about 1530, became a skilled seafarer. She had a large fleet of galleys based in Clew Bay, on Ireland's west coast. Her pirates raided the Irish coast and attacked Atlantic shipping from the 1560s. She negotiated a royal pardon in 1593 and retired.

Word Bank

breakers: waves

galley: a type of boat

plunder: steal from

The countries of Europe were often at war with each other and it became common for seafarers to attack and plunder enemy ships. Whether they were pirates or official privateers, they all became known by the French term, 'corsairs'. Many became popular heroes and some played an important part in history.

St Malo was already a corsair haven when Brittany came under French rule in 1488. Privateers kept up the tradition,

attacking English shipping around the world. Corsair captains such as Réné Duguay-Trouin and Robert Surcouf became heroes.

Klein Hänslein

On a single day in 1573, 33 pirates were executed in Hamburg, Germany. Their captain was called 'Little Jack', or Klein Hänslein. He was the terror of merchant shipping in the North Sea.

The devil's own

In the 1200s, a Flemish monk called Eustace left his monastery to become a soldier. When he was outlawed for murder, he turned pirate and worked the English Channel, first for the English and then for the French. A medieval manuscript shows his grisly end – Eustace was beheaded in a sea battle off Sandwich, Kent.

Questions

1. Draw a line to match each pirate with his/her description. One line has been drawn for you. Draw three more lines.

Grace O'Malley   Beheaded in a sea battle

Eustace, the monk   A corsair captain who became a hero

Klein Hänslein   Escaped to France in a rowing boat

Robert Surcouf   An Irish noblewoman

2. Now copy and complete this table. Put a tick in the correct column to show whether the statements are fact or an opinion (see page 45).

	FACT	OPINION
Piracy was common in the Middle Ages.	_____	_____
Pirates are brave.	_____	_____
Piracy was a fair way to attack enemies.	_____	_____
Eustace was a murderer.	_____	_____
Klein Hänslein means Little Jack.	_____	_____
Pirates deserve to be hanged.	_____	_____

3. Which pirate do you think was the most dangerous? Explain your answer.

Investigations

In pairs or in groups, work through the following tasks to find out how the layout of the extract helps to make the meaning clear.

1. a) Find and write down the main heading of the text.

   b) Why do you think the extract has this heading?

2. a) Find and write down three sub-headings.

   b) How did you find these?

3. Look at the illustrations. These are important because they give you more information. What do the illustrations tell you about:

   a) Grace O'Malley

   b) Eustace

   c) Little Jack

4. Look at the illustration in the middle of the page. Why do you think this illustration is included?

 ## Response

Produce an information leaflet about pirates in the Middle Ages. The information leaflet is for primary children.

- Choose a title for your leaflet.
- Decide which pieces of information you are going to use.
  - Which ones will primary children be interested in?
  - Which ones will they understand?
- What sub-headings will you use?
  - How will you make these clear?
- What illustrations, if any, will you use?
- What different types of print or font will you need if you are using a computer?

Now write your leaflet.

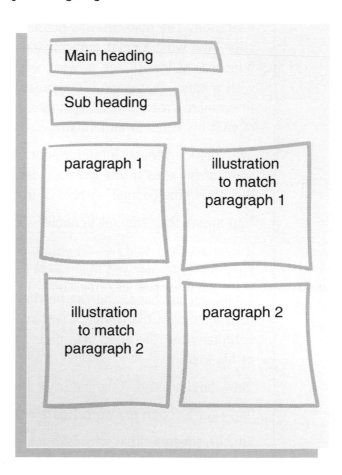

Main heading

Sub heading

| paragraph 1 | illustration to match paragraph 1 |
| illustration to match paragraph 2 | paragraph 2 |

F2 Treasure Island

Treasure Island is one of the most famous pirate stories ever written. The story is told by Jim Hawkins, a young boy who lives and works at the Admiral Benbow Inn, with his mother and father. A stranger, Captain Billy Bones, appears at the inn. The captain rents a room at the inn and pays Jim to keep watch for 'a seafaring man with one leg.'

One evening, Jim's father dies quite suddenly. A few days later, a sinister figure visits the 'Admiral Benbow' looking for the captain.

So things passed until, the day after the funeral, and about three o'clock of a bitter, foggy, frosty afternoon, I was standing at the door for a moment, full of sad thoughts about my father, when I saw someone drawing slowly near along the road. He was plainly blind, for he tapped before him with a stick, and wore a great green shade over his eyes and nose; and he was hunched, as if with age or weakness, and wore a huge old tattered sea-cloak with a hood, that made him appear positively deformed. I never saw in my life a more dreadful-looking figure. He stopped a little from the inn, and, raising his voice in an odd sing-song, addressed the air in front of him:–

'Will any kind friend inform a poor blind man, who has lost the precious sight of his eyes in the gracious defence of his native country, England, and God bless King George! – where or in what part of this country he may now be?'

'You are at the "Admiral Benbow", Black Hill Cove, my good man,' said I.

'I hear a voice,' said he – 'a young voice. Will you give me your hand, my kind young friend, and lead me in?'

I held out my hand, and the horrible, soft-spoken, eyeless creature gripped it in a moment like a vice. I was so much startled that I struggled to withdraw; but the blind man pulled me close up to him with a single action of his arm.

'Now, boy,' he said, 'take me in to the captain.'

'Sir,' said I, 'upon my word I dare not.'

'Oh,' he sneered, 'that's it! Take me in straight, or I'll break your arm.'

And he gave it, as he spoke, a wrench that made me cry out.

'Sir,' said I, 'it is for yourself I mean. The captain is not what he used to be. He sits with a drawn cutlass. Another gentleman—'

'Come, now, march,' interrupted he; and I never heard a voice so cruel, and cold, and ugly as that blind man's. It cowed me more than the pain; and I began to obey him at once, walking straight in at the door and towards the parlour, where our sick old buccaneer was sitting, dazed with rum. The blind man clung close to me, holding me in one iron fist, and leaning almost more of his weight on me than I could carry. 'Lead me straight up to him, and when I'm in view, cry out, "Here's a friend for you, Bill." If you don't, I'll do this;' and with that he gave me a twitch that I thought would have made me faint. Between this and that, I was so utterly terrified of the blind beggar that I forgot my terror of the captain, and as I opened the parlour door, cried out the words he had ordered in a trembling voice.

The poor captain raised his eyes, and at one look the rum went out of him, and left him staring sober. The expression of his face was not so much of terror as of mortal sickness. He made a movement to rise, but I do not believe he had enough force left in his body.

'Now, Bill, sit where you are,' said the beggar. 'If I can't see, I can hear a finger stirring. Business is business. Hold out your right hand. Boy, take his right hand by the wrist, and bring it near to my right.'

We both obeyed him to the letter, and I saw him pass something from the hollow of his hand that held his stick into the palm of the captain's, which closed upon it instantly.

'And now that's done,' said the blind man; and at the words he suddenly left hold of me, and, with incredible accuracy and nimbleness, skipped out of the parlour and into the road, where, as I still stood motionless, I could hear his stick go tap-tap-tapping into the distance.

Questions

1. Choose the correct answer to these questions.

   a) How did Jim know the person who came to the inn was blind?

   i) he walked slowly

   ii) he tapped before him with a stick

   iii) he was hunched.

   b) What did the blind man tell Jim to do?

   i) take him to the captain

   ii) give him his hand

   iii) sit down.

   c) What did the blind man do to the captain?

   i) pinched his arm

   ii) gave him a drink

   iii) put something in his hand.

2. a) What did Jim think of the blind man when he first saw him?

   b) How did the blind man change after he gripped Jim's arm?

3. a) Which of these sentences best describes the blind man.

   i) You feel sorry for him at the end when it says, 'I could hear his stick go tap-tap-tapping'.

   ii) You feel scared of him at the end when it says, 'I could hear his stick go tap-tap-tapping'.

   b) Why have you chosen this sentence?

Investigations

Characterisation

The visitor to the inn was Blind Pew, a very unpleasant character. In pairs, work through the following tasks to find out how Stevenson built up a picture of Blind Pew.

1. What is the most frightening thing about Blind Pew's appearance? Using your copy of the text, mark words or phrases that describe how he looks and make him seem frightening.

   e.g.**he was hunched**

2. Now find and mark four groups of words that describe Blind Pew's voice.

3. Now find and mark four groups of words that show that Jim is frightened of Blind Pew.

4. Find and mark the sentence that shows how the captain feels when he sees Blind Pew.

5. Now write a paragraph explaining why Blind Pew seems frightening. You should comment on:

   - what he looks like
   - what he sounds like
   - how other characters react to him.

Response

After Blind Pew left the inn, the captain died of a heart attack. Later that night, Jim and his mother find a strange packet in his sea chest. Jim had just picked up the packet when he heard the tap-tapping of Blind Pew's stick. He had come back and he was not alone.

Continue the story.

First plan your work. Use these questions to help you:

1. Who is Blind Pew?
2. Who is with him?
3. What do they look like?
4. How do they speak?
5. What do they want?
6. How do Jim and his mother react?
7. What happens at the end?

Check!

Remember to use descriptions of what people look like, how they speak and how others react to them to build up a picture of your characters.

F3 Stories in Art

When sailors came back from their travels they described the strange creatures they had seen. This extract shows some paintings that were done from the descriptions.

Creatures from travellers' stories

Before the invention of modern methods of transport like trains, people travelled the world by boat. These early explorers returned home with stories about the wonderful things they had seen. But some of their descriptions were so amazing that they were hard to believe. It must have been tempting for the travellers to exaggerate their adventures. Or perhaps the memories of their experiences seemed more marvellous when they reached home!

Bestiaries

Some explorers wrote books describing strange foreign animals that they had seen. The books were called bestiaries. They contained descriptions and drawings of the creatures. The pictures were often drawn by an artist, from a traveller's description. Can you imagine how notes about an unusual animal could become an even stranger picture? The first place in each bestiary was usually given to the lion. Descriptions of many real and imagined animals followed. Tired eagles were said to get their strength back by flying near the hot sun, then plunging themselves three times into a fountain.

The whale

The sight of a whale confused and frightened many early sailors. A whale resting near the surface of the sea looked so large that some sailors thought it was an island. This painting from an English bestiary records how striking the sight of a whale must have been. It seems to have an enormous number of fins and tails, and its face looks almost human.

'The Whale' comes from the Ashmole Bestiary.

Stories about dragons

How would you paint a picture of a creature you could never see? Dragons are imaginary creatures, which appear in stories and pictures all over the world. In the East, dragons are seen as powerful creatures who can bring great good fortune as well as bad luck. In Europe, dragons were always described in stories as wicked creatures.

Chinese dragons

According to Chinese stories, the dragon is a magnificent and sacred beast. One description gives it a mane like a lion, horns above its eyes, fins like a fish and a scaly body. It breathes out fire and a pearl rests in the middle of the flames. This dragon can cause rain, wind and storms when it is angry.

Chinese dragons can also bring good fortune. If you look up at the sky during a heavy rainstorm you may catch a glimpse of a dragon. But you can never see the whole of it because it has such a long tail. If you do see the dragon, you will have a long life and great riches. Dragons frequently appear on Chinese porcelain and fabrics, as well as on paintings and scrolls.

European dragons

The dragon in European stories is always seen as an evil monster. It lives in a dark cave and captures people to eat. A dragon can only be killed if it is blinded. Stories tell us about a brave nobleman who kills the dragon and rescues a captured girl. In most stories, the dragon is killed by a hero called Saint George. You can see Saint George fighting the dragon in this painting by the Italian artist Paolo Uccello.

Allegories

A picture like Uccello's is sometimes called an allegory. This means that each character in the story has a special meaning. In European stories, the dragon stands for everything that is evil. The girl represents gentleness and innocence. And the fine and noble hero who rescues her is a sign of all that is good. The allegories describe how goodness defeats wickedness through the story of the dragon, the hero and the girl.

'Saint George and the Dragon' was painted by the Italian artist Paolo Uccello.

Questions

1. Answer these questions:

   a) What sort of transport was used by early explorers?

   b) What were bestiaries?

   c) Why did some sailors think that whales were islands?

   d) What did the Chinese believe that dragons could do when they were angry?

2. In two sentences describe how a European dragon was different to a Chinese dragon?

3. Read the first paragraph again.

   a) What reasons does the writer suggest for the travellers exaggerating their stories?

   b) Why do you think travellers might have exaggerated their stories?

Investigations

Using paragraphs

A paragraph usually contains one key idea which is then developed.

1. How many paragraphs are there in this extract?

2. Write down the key idea of each of the paragraphs.

   > e.g.   Paragraph 1 Explorer's stories

3. Now make notes under each key idea. Use short sentences. Do not include a lot of detail at this stage.

   > e.g.   Paragraph 1 <u>Explorer's stories</u>
   >
   >   travellers came home
   >
   >   had seen wonderful things
   >
   >   told stories

You should now have a plan for this passage.

Allegory

An allegory does not have to be a painting. There are stories which are allegories. The characters and events represent other things.

Write a short story about the painting by Uccello. Use the following plan for your story. In your writing you must make it clear what each character represents. When you have written your story, show it to a partner. See if they can understand the allegory and tell you the message the story gives.

Allegory plan

Paragraph 1   Introduce the girl

Show how she is gentle and kind.

Paragraph 2   Introduce the dragon

Show that he is evil and violent. He enjoys killing all that is good and kind. He captures the girl.

Paragraph 3   Introduce Saint George

Show that he is brave and good. He will fight to save the girl.

Paragraph 4   The fight

It is difficult to destroy evil. The fight must be long and hard. The dragon nearly wins, but Saint George finally kills him and rescues the girl.

 ## Response

Now make a plan for your own information passage. It could be about pirates, using information from earlier on in this section or about other pictures you know about.

- First plan each paragraph. What will be the main topic of each?
- Then add notes about the detail you will add to each paragraph.
- Finally write out the first draft of your information text.

Read your draft and answer the following questions:

1. Are there any spelling, punctuation or grammatical mistakes?
2. Do the paragraphs link together?
3. Is the information clear?
4. Have I used a variety of sentence types?
5. Do I need to add any more detail? Or is there anything that is unnecessary?

Make the changes you need and then write out a final version of your information leaflet.

F4 The Sea

Read this poem aloud before you answer the questions on the next page.

Word Bank

dune: area of sand and grass

The Sea

The sea is a hungry dog,
Giant and grey.
He rolls on the beach all day.
With his clashing teeth and shaggy jaws
Hour upon hour he gnaws
The rumbling, tumbling stones,
And 'Bones, bones, bones, bones!'
The giant sea-dog moans,
Licking his greasy paws.

And when the night wind roars
And the moon rocks in the stormy cloud,
He bounds to his feet and snuffs and sniffs,
Shaking his wet sides over the cliffs,
And howls and hollos long and loud.

But on quiet days in May or June,
When even the grasses on the dune
Play no more their reedy tune,
With his head between his paws
He lies on the sandy shores,
So quiet, so quiet, he scarcely snores.

James Reeves

Questions

1. James Reeves says that the sea is a dog. Find three examples of how the sea is a dog.

2. James Reeves describes the sea at three different times:

in the day time	at night	in the summer

   In what ways is the sea a dog at each of the three times?

3. a) What is your impression of the sea in the first stanza.
      Is the sea rough, powerful, dangerous? Which words tell you?

   b) What is your impression of the sea in the second stanza?
      Is the sea strange, mysterious, comforting? Which words tell you?

   c) What is your impression of the sea in the third stanza?
      Is the sea calm, soothing, refreshing? Which words tell you?

Investigations

When a writer wants to say one thing is *like* another thing, they use a simile. When a writer wants to say one thing *is* another, they use a **metaphor**.

1. James Reeves says the sea is a dog.
   Find examples from the text for each of the following:

   a) the sea is a dog because it is playful

   b) the sea is a dog because it is dangerous

   c) the sea is a dog because it keeps doing the same thing over and over again

   d) the sea is a dog because it is friendly

   e) the sea is a dog because it is calm.

2. How does James Reeves' metaphor help to create a vivid picture of the sea? Choose three phrases from the poem and explain how they help the reader to see the picture.

> e.g.   He bounds to his feet and snuffs and sniffs

This helps the reader to see the waves coming onto the shore as a dog sniffing in the grass around one spot.

Response

You are going to write a poem that compares one thing to another using metaphor.

First choose one of the following topics:

- the sea
- the wind
- clouds in the sky.

Then decide what you are going to compare it to. You can choose one of the following or use your own ideas:

- a horse
- a kitten
- foam.

Now write down a list of the things they have in common.

> e.g.   The sea is a horse because:
>   it can come galloping in very fast
>   it can be friendly
>   it is very strong

When you have a list of things to compare you can start to write your poem.

This extract is taken from a novel which tells the story of a boy called Laurie who was a learner on board a fishing ship.

Raider

Christmas Day out on the fishing grounds. And still no luck. The Iceman was losing his edge. Unthinkable that he should take the Raider home after the other ships and with only half her fishroom filled. Behind the frosty windows of the bridge the crew saw him pacing, pacing, watching the echo sounder, not eating or sleeping. Living on adrenalin. And the tension on board was charged and charged again until the deck, the cabin, the steel plates of the Raider seemed electric with it. As if, if you reached out to touch a bulkhead, it would hiss and crackle with a million volts.

Laurie was being punished. He was crouched by the rail filling needles with twine. You needed both hands to do this. He had no free hand to hold the rail even though the Raider was bucking through heavy seas. But he dared not stop. It was dark and dinner time. But, 'No Christmas dinner,' the mate had told him, 'till you get them needles filled.'

'You, Jonah,' one of the crew had hissed at him. 'This was going to be a record trip. The Iceman's greatest trip ever. More money than we've ever made! He staked his reputation on it. But you held up the trawl. You put Billy out of action. And he's worth twenty of you. A thousand of you!'

Laurie, his hands frozen, couldn't keep up with the rhythm of the gutting team. He'd slowed them down and, worse than that, his gutting knife had slipped into Billy's thigh. Billy couldn't work and now they were scared his blood was poisoned.

'We'll be a joke,' the third hand said, 'when we get back to port. Last and with no fish. The Iceman will be a joke. And all because of you.'

Laurie crouched by the rail, filling needles. His hands were cracked and bleeding with salt-water sores. It was Christmas Day – but he dared not let himself think about that.

Before he sailed he'd planned to keep a journal, a 'Seafarer's Journal'. Write up his adventures on the Arctic Raider, day by day: the first glacier, the first spouting whale, the first volcanic island. The night before he sailed he'd written a long, long entry. But he'd scarcely written anything since.

For a week before he sailed he'd secretly soaked his hands in methylated spirits to harden them. He'd done press-ups and sit-ups in his room to make himself tough and strong.

But he'd started being sick before they'd cleared the lock gates. He'd let a cable slip and almost sheared off the tip of the third hand's skull – neat as topping your breakfast egg. And on his first day, he'd shovelled ice for only an hour in the fishroom before he fell asleep and someone else had to finish the job. As junior deckhand he'd been a total disaster area.

They were having Christmas dinner in the galley. There was warm, fragrant steam coming up through the vents. But out here the ship was icing up. Laurie screwed up his eyes, tried to brush the ice-crystals off his eyelashes. He was swaying, dizzy, tired to the marrow of his bones. He had to jerk his head upright to stop himself falling face down in the basket of wooden needles and going to sleep

His surroundings seemed unreal, shuddering in and out of focus. For a brief moment the engine's whine, the battering waves, the wind, faded into the background and he saw the Raider, iced up like a Christmas cake, with a glittering superstructure and those icicles like tattered crystal flags along the rigging. And the sea around seemed full of silver coins as it too began to freeze.

'Beautiful,' murmured Laurie. 'Beautiful.'

But the Raider plunged down and took a sea and Laurie had to grab the basket to stop it falling over the side.

'Thank God.' He closed his eyes in silent prayer because he'd saved the needles. Then he opened them. This was reality.

Suddenly, Laurie spewed up into the needles. The next one he took out was coated with slime. It slithered from his frozen hands and was lost over the side.

Laurie had to account personally to the mate for every one of the needles in that basket.

In unthinking panic, he leapt up to peer over the rail and at that moment the Raider rolled and tipped him over the side into the dark. His basket of needles followed him. The ship rose up like a cliff face above him and he knew there was no one on deck. No one to see him fall or hear his cries. His only chance was to grab the rail as it came plunging down towards him slowly, slowly like a slow-motion film.

He stretched out both his arms, streaming with water.

Someone did see him fall. The Iceman was on his bridge, looking down. He saw the boy go over the side and when he didn't come back with the next wave he knew he was done for. Two, three minutes, was the most you could survive in that freezing sea and by the time they eased down, turned back, and in the dark – there wasn't a hope in hell, even of finding a body. He would have eased down if there'd been any hope at all. But in the circumstances it would be time wasted.

So the Raider steamed away to the best trip, with the best catches, that the Iceman had ever made. His reputation, in his home port, became even more spectacular. They made up songs about his exploits. Some said he had supernatural powers, because he always knew where to find the fish. Some said he'd sold his soul to the devil.

But the Iceman didn't know everything. He saw a great many things from the bridge. He saw his deckhand fall but he knew nothing of the conscious, clear-minded decision that Laurie took to let go of the rail. Laurie had the rail in his hands and it was taking him up, up again to the deck of the Raider.

He could have saved himself. But he chose not to. Instead Laurie unclenched his fingers, let the rail go – and slipped back into the icy waters.

Questions

1. Put the following pictures in the correct order.

a)

b)

c)

d)

e)

2. a) Which of these words would you use to describe the opening of the text?

funny	unusual	dramatic	descriptive

   b) Explain your answer.

3. Why do you think Laurie chose to let go of the rail?

4. a) Which of these characters does Susan Gates, the writer of *Raider*, have the most sympathy for?

   i) the Mate

   ii) Billy

   iii) Laurie

   iv) the Iceman

   b) Explain your answer.

Investigations

Narrator's point of view

The narrator of this story is not one of the characters. He is outside the action, watching and describing what is happening.

When the narrator is outside the action, he can show us the action from different people's point of view.

1. Read the first paragraph of the passage again.

    a) Whose point of view is being given here?

    b) Who does the 'you' in the final sentence refer to?

2. Read the second paragraph.

    a) Whose point of view is being given here?

    b) How does he feel?

    c) What words and phrases in this paragraph tell you this?

3. Read the whole passage again.

    a) When does the point of view change again?

    b) Who does it change to?

    c) Why does the point of view change here?

The changing of point of view is very useful because it means we can hear the true feelings of different characters.

In this passage we learnt that:

- Laurie chose to die

- the Iceman would have gone back if there had been a chance.

4. a) Write down the sentences that tell us each of these facts.

    b) Why do you think we might need to know them?

Response

The skipper of the Arctic Raider, the Iceman, would have had to write a report giving the details of Laurie's death. This would only give his point of view of the accident.

Write the report in short clear sentences. The report should say:

- what happened
- when it happened
- how it happened
- why it happened.

Check!

Remember to write from the Iceman's point of view and to make up a convincing reason for why the accident happened.

Test Yourself!

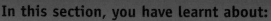

In this section, you have learnt about:
- layout
- characterisation
- using paragraphs
- metaphor
- allegories
- narrator's point of view.

Answer one of the following questions to show that you have understood what you have learnt.

1. Write a leaflet giving information about some of the pictures you have seen in this section for other users of this book. Remember to lay out your text in the most helpful way for your reader and to use paragraphs to make your leaflet clear.

2. Write a short story of your own about an accident at sea. As you write, remember what you have learnt about characterisation and point of view.